Praise for *This*

"This book is a treasure, a feast, an oasis. Ivan M. Granger's profound gift for selecting the kind of poetry that lights up the cave of the heart and melts the boundaries between the soul and the Divine is fully met by his lucid reflections on the soul-transfiguring power of each piece in this magnificent collection."

MIRABAI STARR
author of *God of Love: A Guide to the Heart
of Judaism, Christianity & Islam*
and *Caravan of No Despair: A Memoir of Loss and Transformation*

"Ivan M. Granger writes as though God is looking over his shoulder. He inspires appreciation of the literature of awakening as he inspires the reader's own heart awakening. This anthology features poetic masterpieces from around the world, each one revealing the profound interconnectedness of all things. The comments accompanying each selection are direct and engaging, unfolding layers of meaning, further enhancing the themes of union, interconnection, and non-separation."

JERRY KATZ
editor of *One: Essential Writings on Nonduality*
www.nonduality.org

"In the midst of the tumult and heartbreak of history's headlines, Ivan M. Granger has tended his online "Teahouse," the Poetry Chaikhana, where countless lucky sojourners can share a moment of sanity through the communion of sacred poetry. In *This Dance of Bliss*, his latest anthology, he graces us with mystical poems from across time and around the world that return us to the placeless, timeless truth of being. Each page offers a doorway of words into the miraculous beyond words. Each of his companion meditations is a key to that door. These days I hold these poems closer than ever, and they are life-saving."

KIM ROSEN
author of *Saved by a Poem: The Transformative Power of Words*

"Ivan M. Granger's work is *seva*, selfless service offered joyously for the upliftment of all. We as readers are invited to step out of the confines of the ordinary mind and into the dance of bliss unfolding in this collection. Ivan's careful selection of poems, his translations of some, and his commentaries and reflections on them, all serve to invite us into the unitive experience that is the dance of creation, the dance of life, *This Dance of Bliss!*"

LAWRENCE EDWARDS, PH.D.
founder and director of the Anam Cara Meditation Foundation
author of *Kali's Bazaar* (as Kalidas),
The Soul's Journey: Guidance from the Divine Within,
and *Awakening Kundalini: The Path to Radical Freedom*
www.thesoulsjourney.com

"I highly recommend Ivan M. Granger's unique anthology for its variety, inclusiveness, philosophical depth, emotional integrity— and that subtle electric current we call *inspiration* as it flares in our senses. His contribution here is outstanding. Through this poetry the spirit gains an education like no other."

JAY RAMSAY
co-editor with Andrew Harvey of *Diamond Cutters: Visionary Poets in America, Britain & Oceania*,
author of *Pilgrimage: A Journey to Love Island*

"In this rich and profound book Ivan M. Granger is your mature mystic guide, drawing out the inherent wisdom in each poem and bringing deep relevance to our contemporary minds and hearts. I will be highly recommending *This Dance of Bliss* to everyone I know."

MEGHAN DON
author of *The New Divine Feminine: Spiritual Evolution for a Woman's Soul*
www.GnosticGrace.com

Also from Poetry Chaikhana

The Longing in Between: Sacred Poetry from Around the World
  Edited with Commentary by Ivan M. Granger

Real Thirst: Poetry of the Spiritual Journey
  Poems & Translations by Ivan M. Granger

Gathering Silence
  Sayings by Ivan M. Granger with Collages by Rashani Réa

Marrow of Flame: Poems of the Spiritual Journey
  by Dorothy Walters

THIS DANCE OF BLISS

This Dance of Bliss

Ecstatic Poetry from Around the World

A Poetry Chaikhana Anthology

Edited with Commentary by
Ivan M. Granger

POETRY CHAIKHANA

www.poetry-chaikhana.com

ISBN: 0-9854679-7-5

ISBN-13: 978-0-9854679-7-5

To

*the helpers, teachers, and fellow travelers
we meet along the way.*

CONTENTS

Introduction

My father was a poet, so poetry was part of my world from a young age. But I didn't take poetry seriously. The poetry I read was, well, rather boring to me. I thought of poetry as belonging to my father's world, an academic world.

That was my relationship with poetry well into adulthood—that is, until poetry took up residence at the center of my life.

In the early 2000s, I was living with my wife on the island of Maui. It was a beautiful time in my life, but aimless. I was just doing work to get by, with no career to speak of. I was cut off from the world, by distance and by choice.

A friend sent me a series of talks by the poet David Whyte on cassette tape, and I went for long drives along Maui's meandering country roads, through the tall sugar cane fields and among the rows of spiky pineapple plants, listening to David Whyte's molasses accent as he recited poetry and told stories about brilliant and troubled poets, like Antonio Machado and Anna Akhmatova.

During this time in my life, my one goal was spiritual growth. That was my only identity. And it was in total disarray.

Christmas came, and I had just broken with the spiritual group that had been my focus for the previous ten years. No great drama instigated my leaving. I simply knew it was no longer right for me. But walking away left me adrift. I was still engaged in intense spiritual practice, but it had lost its context. Should I continue with the same meditation, the same prayers and fasts? What did they mean without the specific spiritual worldview in which I first adopted them? The holidays only emphasized my disorientation.

I came to a profound personal confrontation. For the first time I really saw myself. It was a terrifying moment. I dropped all pretense and projection, all the fantasies of who I thought I was or might become. I just looked at myself plainly, as I was.

What I saw wasn't terribly impressive. I could see that I was basically a good-hearted person, but largely ineffectual. I remember thinking with a sad chuckle, "I'm just a likeable flake." What truly surprised me, though, was the thought that followed, which was, "That's really okay."

New Year's Day came and went, while I hovered in that open limbo state. This combination began to ferment in my mind, the poetry and the personal crisis.

In early January it all converged and—POW!—I was catapulted into an ecstatic stillness. Everything about me and my world came to a complete stop. The person I thought of as "Ivan" disappeared. It was as if some undefined, wide-open awareness was quietly witnessing the world through my eyes. An indescribable joy bubbled up inside me. The entire world was an intangible outline sketched upon a golden-white radiance, and I was a ghost happily lost in that light.

I spent days hardly speaking, with a crooked grin plastered across my face.

I could see that I was unsettling my wife, so I made a game of it. I pretended to be Ivan. I resumed my work schedule. I walked our dogs. I cleaned the small house we rented. But everything shone.

That's when I started to write in a journal, trying to describe what I was experiencing, how the world was changed, how I was changed. How I was finally myself. But what really wanted to come out was—poetry!

As I wrote more poetry, I found a certain metaphoric language naturally emerging: water and honey and wine, moon and sun and light…

It was then that I came across books of sacred poetry by St. John of the Cross, Rumi, Abu-Said Abil-Kheir, and Ramprasad. Their words were electrifying. They whispered to me as intimate companions. And I noticed that they used the same language of wine and moonlight.

I became hungry for more. I started rummaging through the island's used bookstores for more poetry collections. I scanned anthologies for new names and voices. Sufi poets, Hindu poets, Buddhist poets, Christian poets.

I realized that there was a rich world heritage of sacred poetry, hundreds of poets, thousands of poets, singing songs of the divine—and I had heard of none of them before. Most commentaries I found were dry, scholarly analyses, which have their value, but lack real insight. It was frustrating to find such profound wisdom and ecstatic joy, yet have it thought to be significant only to historians and religious scholars. The few poems that reached the general public were seen as merely beautiful, while the inner experiences they expressed were out of focus.

Gathering this poetry together, I immersed myself in it. I began to organize it, looking for connected themes and language.

In 2004, my wife and I returned to the mainland, moving back to Colorado. Soon after we were settled, I launched a website to encourage exploration of this visionary poetry without academic jargon, helping readers find their own doorway into the heart of this amazing poetry.

This is how the Poetry Chaikhana was born.

—⁓—

I am always asked, what the word "chaikhana" means.

The short answer is that a chaikhana is a tea house, *chai* being the word for tea in many parts of the world.

The inevitable second question is, what is a "poetry chaikhana"? What does poetry, especially sacred poetry, have to do with tea?

The act of sipping tea has a contemplative quality to it, which, I think, suits this sort of poetry well. And a teahouse is a public space. It is a place of community and sharing. I think of sacred poetry as a solitary pleasure that is, at the same time, meant to be shared with friends and family. Its insight and inspiration naturally filters out into the wider society through the spoken word and books passed along.

But there is a more personal reason for the unusual name. I was inspired by a Sufi story I came across several years ago—

The Story of Tea

Long ago, few outside the fabled land of Chin had heard of the drink called "tea." What little was known was rumor and speculation. But tales spread of a celestial drink that clarified the mind and calmed the spirit.

Many tried to discover this magical nectar.

The great lords of the Kingdom of Might sent an embassy to the Emperor of the Chin. Standing before him, the ambassadors boldly demanded tea for their kingdom. The Emperor readily assented and presented them with many sacks of fine tea leaves. But, on departing the royal city, when the ambassadors saw the common people drinking tea in the streets, they cast their heavy sacks into the gutter and returned home empty handed, convinced that they had been cheated, for a drink that touched the lips of commoners was not worthy of the great lords of the Kingdom of Might. And had not the Emperor given away this "tea" too quickly, without negotiation and counter demands? Surely it was not the true celestial drink.

The Republic of Philosophers held a convocation of scholars to gather together all that was known of tea in their land. They consulted ancient books and travelers' tales, but their conclave quickly fragmented into factions. Some cited irreproachable sources that clearly described tea as a liquid, while others held up authoritative commentaries that declared tea to be an herb. The black party could not agree with the green party over the color of tea, not to mention those radicals in the ochre party! And then sub-factions within each argued that its flavor was sweet, no bitter, bitter-sweet, or, rather, sweetly bitter. All the while, the rationalists argued that such a varied substance could not possibly exist. The most learned among them, a sage who had spent his long life studying these many questions, concluded that, for all their voluminous knowledge about tea, he and his fellow philosophers knew nothing of the celestial drink.

In the Confederation of Skill, the most brilliant and subtle alchemists dedicated their lives and their fortunes to unlocking the celestial drink. They filled their laboratories with every herb and liquid known. They calcinated and dissolved. They separated and conjoined. They fermented and distilled and coagulated. And they sampled each and every substance. Many were poisoned. Many died. All were disappointed. Their ingenuity could not remedy the fact that tea had never been brought to their land.

In the Principalities of Belief—they had tea! They had a single bag of tea. Of course, no one drank it. No one knew how. Their tea was carried in a grand procession every year throughout the land. Their princes built temples to house the tea as it was carried in its annual circuit around the country. Priests delivered thundering sermons on the supreme perfection of their satchel of tea. Congregations sang hymns to it. The provinces fought wars among themselves to prove their dedication to it. But nobody drank the tea. No one knew how.

Then a traveler came among them, a man of wisdom. He spoke with a quiet voice, but his words rang throughout the land. He said, *Toss your bag of tea into boiling water! Drink it down to the last drop!*

Blasphemy! cried the priests.

Heresy! wailed the pious.

This man, this outsider, was preaching the destruction of their sacred tea! They had him arrested, they beat him, they slew him.

But before this wise man was killed, seekers came to him to learn in secret, and he taught them in secret. They obtained tea by hidden channels. And in hidden places they brewed the celestial drink, drinking and sharing it in secret.

Long after the wise man's death, sincere seekers continued to gather privately to delight in the celestial drink. This humble practice spread from neighbor to neighbor and from land to land. As they passed the precious liquid amongst themselves, they repeated the words of their teacher: *He who tastes, knows.*

Travelers brought tea with them on their journeys. Whenever a pilgrim paused to rest, he would brew tea and offer it to his companions. This is how the chaikhanas, the tea houses, came into being as places of rest and renewal along the Silk Road.

Centuries of argument and theory were dispelled with a single sip of the celestial drink.

Those who tasted, knew.

Inspired by a story told by Hamadani

IMG

I hope the poems and thoughts in this Poetry Chaikhana anthology bring a hint of that celestial drink to your lips.

These are poems to be tasted. They are meant to be imbibed until we feel awarmth in the belly and sweetness in the heart—and we find ourselves swept up in this dance of bliss.

He who tastes, knows.

——∿∿——

A hundred flowers in spring

A hundred flowers in spring, the moon in autumn,
the breeze in summer, in winter snow.
When the mind is unclouded,
this is the best season of life.

Wu Men

IMG

A hundred flowers in spring ～

A hundred flowers in spring, the moon in autumn,
the breeze in summer, in winter snow.

The shifting seasons against the living canvas of the world invite
us to notice the cycles of life, how everything flows and changes
and returns again. Because the world is filled with life, nothing
remains the same. Everything grows and changes and comes
around again renewed.

When the mind is unclouded...

Watching that flow, we witness such beauty. But we can only
truly see it when we let the mind quiet and become clear.

In such moments, a fullness of the soul overwhelms us. We
become creatures of silent delight, content and complete in
ourselves as we watch the parade of life's seasons move past,
leaving us fully alive in this very moment.

...this is the best season of life.

———ᴠᴠᴠ———

Annunciation

Even if I don't see it again—nor ever feel it
I know it is—and that if once it hailed me
it ever does—

And so it is myself I want to turn in that direction
not as toward a place, but it was a tilting
within myself,

as one turns a mirror to flash the light to where
it isn't—I was blinded like that—and swam
in what shone at me

only able to endure it by being no one and so
specifically myself I thought I'd die
from being loved like that.

                                                        Marie Howe

Annunciation ∿

Even if I don't see it again—nor ever feel it
I know it is—and that if once it hailed me
it ever does—

That flash of insight the poet speaks of, that annunciation, is
more than a new way for us to look at things. When the deepest
realizations come upon us, we are transformed. We see that the
world is not as we imagined, and neither are we.

This new view of reality carries a hidden challenge, however. Our
natural instinct is to try to hold that holistic vision in our
awareness and neatly situate ourselves within it. But it is not a
thing to be held and defined. Sometimes the vision stays.
Sometimes it comes and goes and returns again. Sometimes it is
but a quick glimpse, the beckoning of future enlightenment. But
once encountered, whether brief or lasting, it is undeniably real.
We have been touched. Some deep-seated part of the self now
knows beyond question that a greater reality exists.

With time and practice, we learn to seek not the vision itself, but
the wholeness it illuminates. We learn to no longer grasp at
reality as something outside ourselves yet to be discovered and
claimed. It is already there within us. And it continuously calls to
us.

And so it is myself I want to turn in that direction
not as toward a place, but it was a tilting
within myself,

We instinctively reorient our whole selves toward that shining
reality. We tilt our faces to be awash in its light. Unable to grasp
it, we let it flood us instead. Immersed in that flash of
illumination, we swim upstream, drawn to its brilliant source...

...I was blinded like that—and swam
in what shone at me

I especially love the poem's closing lines—

only able to endure it by being no one and so
specifically myself I thought I'd die
from being loved like that.

The poet has it just right. We only remain aligned and awake in that moment of insight when we become "no one." Yet by freeing ourselves from the surface ego-self, somehow, inexplicably, we become exactly and fully as we are, "so specifically myself."

Wrapped in such a delicious flood of love, can that old self survive? Does it even want to?

—◆◆—

Grand is the Seen

Grand is the seen, the light, to me—grand are the sky and stars,
Grand is the earth, and grand are lasting time and space,
And grand their laws, so multiform, puzzling, evolutionary;
But grander far the unseen soul of me, comprehending,
    endowing all those,
Lighting the light, the sky and stars, delving the earth, sailing the
    sea,
(What were all those, indeed, without thee, unseen soul? of what
    amount without thee?)
More evolutionary, vast, puzzling, O my soul!
More multiform far—more lasting thou than they.

Walt Whitman

Grand is the Seen ∿

Grand is the seen, the light, to me—grand are the sky and stars,
Grand is the earth, and grand are lasting time and space,
And grand their laws, so multiform, puzzling, evolutionary...

Our wisdom traditions, both East and West, often encourage us to dismiss the material world in favor of an inner reality, whether that's the world of the intellect and ideas or the realm of spirit.

Whitman has the balance right, I think. First, he acknowledges the wondrous "seen" world of beauty and complexity that invites our awareness to explore and expand.

But then he recognizes the soul as something greater still...

But grander far the unseen soul of me, comprehending, endowing all
those...

The soul alone is aware of the world. Without the soul's awareness, all of creation is merely dense existence. The infusion of consciousness into the world is what makes it possible to witness that material reality as beauty, as immensity, as perilous, as life-filled, as home. All of manifest existence is a grand space, but it is only through perception that it has its grandeur.

(What were all those, indeed, without thee, unseen soul? of what amount
without thee?)

The expansive, lovely, occasionally dangerous spaces we witness in the natural world, tell us something of the human soul that perceives them. The ways in which we treat those wild spaces also tell us what we think of the wild and unexplored realms within ourselves.

More evolutionary, vast, puzzling, O my soul!
More multiform far—more lasting thou than they.

As wide as is the natural world that houses us, the soul is larger still. This can be an overwhelming realization. Our reflex is to shrink our self-image, imagining ourselves to be small and uninteresting, residing within a safely mapped world. Mapped though our world may be, it is not understood as thoroughly as we imagine. And neither are we. Better to embrace the immensity we are as living witnesses to the grandeur we inhabit.

—⁓—

Laus Trinitati

Praise to the Trinity!
     the music and the life,
     the mother of all,
  the life within life.
Praise sung by the angelic host,
     the wondrous secret splendor,
     hidden from the human eye, and yet
  alive everywhere.

Hildegard von Bingen

IMG

Laus Trinitati ～

> *the music and the life,*
> *the mother of all,*
> *the life within life.*

We are prone to be poor witnesses. When we take a walk in the woods, for example, what do we notice? Trees. Bushes and undergrowth. Grasses in the clearings. Birds singing and darting about. Perhaps a rabbit or a deer, if we are lucky. We see all this movement and greenery, and we call it "life." We then imagine that life is tangible, measurable, easily watched, described, and categorized. But these things—plants, animals, ourselves, even the land, the waters, and the sky—these are not life itself, they are its expression.

Life is the intangible essence that animates and awakens living beings. It is the urge to grow and to flower. It is the will to move and to survive. It is the intelligence behind the eyes. Within every blade of grass and animal artery runs this secret sap. Behind every glance and leap and flutter circulates this hidden breath.

It is this "secret splendor," this inner radiance "hidden from the human eye" that is the real life. Amidst the endless diversity of beings there is but a single life. And though it is hidden, it is manifest everywhere.

Elsewhere Hildegard von Bingen refers to this flow of universal life as God's "greening" of the world.

This vital presence has a quiet thrum to it, a vibration—a sound. The divine outpouring is also music. God is the rhythm of existence. And we, together with all things, are part of the chorus. Our very being is a song of praise.

Notice how easily Hildegard sidesteps the patriarchy of medieval Christian thought and addresses this vision of the Trinity as "the mother of all." For her, the Divine is nurturing, everywhere present, nourishing as milk to the newborn, life-giving. Naming it mother feels right.

—⁓—

The fruits are ripened

Give Me

O Lord, give me a heart
I can pour out in thanksgiving.
Give me life
So I can spend it
Working for the salvation of the world.

Ansari

English version by Andrew Harvey

Give Me ∿

These words come to us from a devout Muslim Sufi, but they could just as easily have been spoken by a Catholic liberation theologian, a Buddhist peace worker, a Hindu karma yogi, a Protestant homeless advocate, or any sincere soul striving to be of service within the world.

Notice that Shaikh Ansari gives us two parallel prayers which balance each other.

The first entreaty—

> *O Lord, give me a heart*
> *I can pour out in thanksgiving.*

—addresses the interior state. He asks for a heart, seeking to awaken the life and compassion at the core of his being. It is a prayer of centering, of coming to know the heart, and allowing that inner self to flow out into the world.

This outpouring of the heart naturally expresses itself through gratitude and thanksgiving. Regardless of whatever great accomplishments we may achieve, the real gift we bring to the world is our heart.

I am reminded of that wonderful quote by Mother Teresa in which she says to a group of wealthy donors, "Money is not enough, money can be got, but they need your hearts to love them." Every problem and instance of suffering in this world needs our engaged hearts, not merely a mechanical solution. This is the heart Ansari asks for, one which is full and eager to offer itself to the world.

Next, Ansari turns that awareness outward through action:

> *Give me life*
> *So I can spend it*
> *Working for the salvation of the world.*

He asks for life that he may be of service.

The term "salvation" has been abducted by pietists who equate salvation with subscribing to their specific belief system. Despite what is thundered from the pulpits and *minbars*, salvation has

15

little to do with belief or which group one joins. It is about the easing of pain, the renewal of hope, and a deepening relationship with truth. On a social level, this is best expressed through selfless service. On the spiritual level, working for salvation is about humbly peeling away the obstructions that keep individuals and the world as a whole from recognizing their innate beauty and divine nature.

Service in the world can be seen as a ritual, an outward enactment of an inner process. We may help one person or a hundred or a thousand, but suffering continues. The numbers game leads to discouragement. Yet with each kind act, small or great, we open our eyes a little more, we become more connected, and more and more we discover the true self at rest within. Acts of kindness and service minimize suffering and loneliness for others while ritually reaffirming the living heart within ourselves.

With this poem's two combined prayers, Ansari reminds us that when we discover the true heart within, it naturally flows out into the world. And when we pour ourselves out for the healing of the world, we rediscover wholeness within.

—⁓—

The Lion, the Wolf, and the Fox

A lion went hunting one day and brought along a wolf and a fox as companions.

They were all excellent hunters and by the end of the day the team had caught an ox, an ibex, and a hare.

The wolf was already hungrily eying their prey, so the lion magnanimously told him, "Wolf, divide up this abundance between us in any way you like."

The wolf, though hungry enough to eat the ox himself, decided it was safest to offer the largest prize to the lion. He claimed the ibex for himself, and handed the smallest, the hare, to the fox. The wolf licked his chops in anticipation, when the lion roared:

"Wolf! How dare you talk of 'mine' and 'yours'!" With a single swipe from his mighty paw, the lion slew the wolf.

The lion calmed himself, and then turned to the fox. With a toothy smile, he said, "Fox, divide up this abundance between us in any way you like."

The fox, being no fool, immediately said that the entire catch belonged to the lion.

The lion rumbled in satisfaction, and said, "Fox, you are no longer a fox! You are myself. The entire bounty is yours!"

Mevlana Jelaluddin Rumi

IMG

The Lion, the Wolf, and the Fox ~

I imagine Rumi laughing with delight as he tells this story. But beneath its sly humor, this tale hides layers of meaning.

The lion is used repeatedly in Sufi writings as a symbol for God, the mighty lord of creation. The lion brings a wolf and a fox with him on a hunting expedition to gather the bounty of his realm.

They catch an ox, an ibex, and a hare. Each of these animals has a symbolic meaning in the story. The ox, like Taurus the Bull in western astrology, represents sensuality and the earth. The ibex represents wildness, uncontained and unrestricted movement. The hare embodies fear, timidity.

The lion then invites the wolf to divide up their catch.

The wolf, representing hunger and avarice, wants to gorge himself on the ox, sensuality, but reluctantly offers that largest of the animals to the lion. Instead, the wolf claims the second largest animal, the ibex, wildness, for himself. Finally, he offers the hare to the smallest in their party, the fox. This seems a logical and, one would think, safe division.

But the lion surprises us by killing the wolf. The lion knows that all the lands and all the bounty they contain rightfully belong to him. For the wolf to presume that he has a right to any of it only to satisfy his greed is to forget that everything always belongs to God alone. The wolf, having forgotten that he too is a part of the lion's undivided kingdom, sees the world in terms of "yours" and "mine," imagining that reality is divisible into portions that can be possessed. In his greed, he can only know the dualistic experience, and this misperception always leads to death.

Finally, the lion invites the fox to divide up their bounty. The fox, representing the cunning mind that can potentially lead to deeper awareness, sees clearly that the only way to avoid death is to abandon all greed. He further recognizes that the bounty of creation cannot be divided or possessed. Acknowledging all of this, and in humility before the overpowering might of the lion, the fox wisely declares that all the bounty they have gathered belongs to the lion alone.

Satisfied, the lion surprises the fox by handing him the entire catch undivided. As the fox acknowledges the indivisible nature of reality, he is surprised to find that he has mastered the failings symbolized by their prey. In this moment of insight, he discovers that he himself is not separate from the lion. The fox, the individual mind, is, at the same time, one with the universal whole. It is only with this selfless recognition that one can properly enjoy the undivided bounty of creation.

> *"Fox, you are no longer a fox! You are myself. The entire bounty is yours!"*

—⁓—

Within this body
breathes the secret essence.
Within this body
beats the heart of the Vedas.

Within this body
shines the entire Universe,
    so the saints say.

Hermits, ascetics, celibates—
all are lost
seeking Him
    in endless guises.

Seers and sages perfectly parrot
the scriptures and holy books,
    blinded by knowledge.

Their pilgrimage,
    and fasting,
    and striving
        but delude.
Despite their perfect practice,
they discover no destination.

Only the saints
who know the body's heart
have attained the Ultimate, O Tulsi.

Realize this and you've found your freedom
    (while teachers trapped in tradition
    know only the mirage
        in the mirror.)

Tulsi Sahib

IMG

20

Within this body ∿

This poem cuts through the problems inherent in religious
fundamentalism—

> *Seers and sages perfectly parrot*
> *the scriptures and holy books,*
> *blinded by knowledge.*

It deflates the fixation on practice and ritual—

> *Their pilgrimage,*
> *and fasting,*
> *and striving*
> *but delude.*

This is not to say that we need never study sacred texts or that
we should ignore traditional spiritual forms. The problem is that
it is easy to forget what their true purpose is. Sacred writings and
religious practice, these are reminders to us to turn inward and
discover the true heart that shines within each of us.

> *Within this body*
> *breathes the secret essence.*
> *Within this body*
> *beats the heart of the Vedas.*

> *Within this body*
> *shines the entire Universe,*
> *so the saints say.*

If we merely memorize words or bow down in the prescribed
forms of prayer, even if we do it perfectly, we are in danger of
idolizing the trappings of religion without making the journey to
the heart.

This spiritual oversight is the reason that fundamentalists of
every religion express so much anger. The fundamentalist
mindset represents the desire to set the flailing individual
securely within a strict definition of faith. There may be sincere
effort, even significant changes in behavior and lifestyle, along
with the forging of close community ties, but real transformation
remains elusive along that path. The problem is that

fundamentalism is concerned with the outer forms of religion. Adhering to them is not the same as making the inner journey.

> *Despite their perfect practice,*
> *they discover no destination.*

Even when the religious rules are carefully followed, fundamentalists find only frustration. This is exactly the opposite of what is expected, and a reason must be found to explain away the failure.

The instinct within these communities is to blame the imperfections of the world for preventing their deserved spiritual joy. The fundamentalist's pain becomes self-righteous anger, which is assumed to be God's anger at an ungodly world.

This creates a terrible bind in which the individual cannot experience spiritual relief until society is forced into compliance. The more desperate these souls become for release from their pain, the more violently they try to enforce their vision upon society in the hopes that they will finally appease God and find freedom.

This is such a tragedy since all that is necessary is to humbly journey inward and open one's heart in order to discover the inexhaustible joy already there.

> *Only the saints*
> *who know the body's heart*
> *have attained the Ultimate, O Tulsi.*

We should study, yes, and strive. But of even more importance is the journey within to discover the heart's luminous secret.

That is the fundamental truth. That is the real fundamentalism.

> *Realize this and you've found your freedom*

—◊—

The fruits are ripened, dipped in fire, cooked
and tested by the earth. The law is this:
that all must wind and curl inward like snakes—
prophetic, dreaming
upon the hills of heaven, with much held
on hunched shoulders, like bundled
branches. But the pathways
are perilous. For the chained elements
and the old laws of earth,
like errant horses, run astray, and always out
beyond the boundaries they go, longing. So much
must be borne in steadfastness.
Forward, backward—neither way
will we look. Instead, we learn to live rocking
like a boat on the sea.

Friedrich Holderlin

IMG

23

The fruits are ripened ∽

This poem by Holderlin is visionary and a bit haunting. Phrases like "the chained elements" tell us that the poet is using the language of alchemy, with its ideas of the perfectibility of the world—and the soul—through transformation and the release of its inner essence.

Let's explore this poem with that alchemical perspective in mind.

> *The fruits are ripened, dipped in fire, cooked...*

Ripening, while natural, is at times painful, for it is a pathway of growth and change. The young hard fruit knows only its greenness. To soften and fill with sweet juice requires leaving the old self behind, yielding into an unknown future self.

Similarly, when food is cooked, it must go through searing heat to draw out its flavor. But once cooked, it is complete, ready. The cookfire is the alchemical fire beneath the crucible. It is the heat that purifies and refines, the intensity of life that draws out our spiritual essence, making us ready.

> *...and tested by the earth.*

This is an odd phrase. We don't typically "test" our food, and what would it mean to test it "by the earth"? But by reading these lines through an alchemical lens, we understand that we ourselves are the food being ripened and cooked. It is our own souls that will be tested and strengthened by the world's rough handling.

> *The law is this:*
> *that all must wind and curl inward like snakes—*
> *prophetic, dreaming*
> *upon the hills of heaven...*

These lines evoke in my mind the vision of a cave painting with spirals and creatures turning in on themselves. All things turn inward to their center, hungering to know their very nature. In discovering that inner landscape, they encounter "the hills of heaven."

I read this poem as a meditation on the struggle of the spiritual seeker engaged in worldly life. Holderlin speaks of shouldering heavy loads and a longing for escape.

So much
must be borne in steadfastness.

The spiritually-minded incline toward an otherworldliness that can make one uniquely vulnerable. The intensity of life experiences can overwhelm and disrupt, making a quick heavenly escape enticing. But we must remember that ripening is patient work, a process of inner opening while interacting with the wider environment.

The challenge is to develop steadiness and the strength to endure our ripening process, letting go of our hardness and old bitterness, while awakening new vision and the sweetness within. Real ripeness requires not escape, but presence and a harmony with the rhythms of life.

Instead, we learn to live rocking
like a boat on the sea.

—⁓—

Fasting

There's hidden sweetness in the stomach's emptiness.
We are lutes, no more, no less. If the soundbox
is stuffed full of anything, no music.
If the brain and belly are burning clean
with fasting, every moment a new song comes out of the fire.
The fog clears, and new energy makes you
run up the steps in front of you.
Be emptier and cry like reed instruments cry.
Emptier, write secrets with the reed pen.
When you're full of food and drink, Satan sits
where your spirit should, an ugly metal statue
in place of the Kaaba. When you fast,
good habits gather like friends who want to help.
Fasting is Solomon's ring. Don't give it
to some illusion and lose your power,
but even if you have, if you've lost all will and control,
they come back when you fast, like soldiers appearing
out of the ground, pennants flying above them.
A table descends to your tents,
Jesus' table.
Expect to see it, when you fast, this table
spread with other food, better than the broth of cabbages.

Rumi

English version by Coleman Barks

26

Fasting ∽

There's hidden sweetness in the stomach's emptiness.
We are lutes, no more, no less. If the soundbox
is stuffed full of anything, no music.

Fasting is something we're not too comfortable with in the affluent West. Even though all religions, including Christianity and Judaism, have ancient traditions of fasting, we don't generally have a well-developed sense of what spirituality has to do with food—or its avoidance.

Even in contemporary spiritual teachings, we commonly hold the notion that all we must do is change our thinking and transformation occurs. But the results of that approach are spotty. One reason is that mind is much more than thoughts, and transforming the mind requires deeper work. Thoughts are built on ingrained energetic currents. For real transformation to occur, we have to get down to those underlying patterns. Very often this requires not merely changing our thoughts but tunneling beneath them. This is the purpose of spiritual practice.

Fasting is a universal way to clear the mind and confront those underlying energies in the awareness.

But why? What does food have to do with any of this?

We are not two things, a mind separate from a body, or even a mind that inhabits a body. The mind and body interpenetrate one another. If the body is injured, that physical pain demands attention, affecting the awareness. The state of the body impacts the clarity and focus of the mind. Feeding the body pure, healthy foods in general, and periodically allowing it to rest from the tiring work of digestion can profoundly free up energies for the awareness to tap into.

Here's something else we are not taught: Food is a drug. Does that sound bizarre to you? Of course, normal foods are not literally hallucinogenic. But all foods are mind-altering to a degree. Every food we eat affects consciousness in some way.

We use food to control emotions. We eat to shift moods and change awareness. Think of the instinct to grab a pint of ice cream from the freezer after a devastating breakup. Everything, even a salad, affects consciousness in some way. The resulting psychic shift caused by eating can be relatively positive or negative. It can help us to feel solid and grounded or spacey and unfocused. It can tantalize the senses, bring us feelings of satisfaction, or leave us agitated. None of this is necessarily bad, but we must understand how profoundly food affects our awareness so that we may utilize food wisely... and occasionally consume no food at all.

A fascinating thing happens when we fast as part of a spiritual practice: After we ease past the initial psychic tension and the body moves through its discomfort, the mind naturally settles and grows quiet. So much of the agitation of the mind arises from the foods we eat.

Recognizing this, food and fasting become an important aspect of spiritual practice.

> *The fog clears, and new energy makes you*
> *run up the steps in front of you.*

The first few times I tried to do a one-day fast, I was frankly terrified. I knew intellectually that a healthy human body can go for days without food, no problem. Many times in the past I had forgotten to eat breakfast, and it was no big deal, but on a day when I intentionally decided to fast, I'd be sweating and panicky by mid-morning.

It took me a while to understand that fasting, even a mild fast, is a confrontation with death. We are not just choosing to rest from feeding the body, we are also refusing to feed the demands of the ego. When the ego's demands are not being met, its illusory nature begins to be revealed. The ego perceives this as the threat of death—which it is, its own death, the slow revelation of the ego's nonexistence. When we identify with the ego, we feel that threat of death personally, and become fearful. Even a simple, safe fast can become an ordeal until we embrace the full spiritual undertaking it represents.

How does one have a desire and just sit with it, without attempting to immediately satisfy it? That can be a frightening question.

With a little practice, we discover that what we typically assume to be physical hunger is actually mental hunger. For well-fed modern individuals, it can take days, literally days, for true physical hunger to arise. The hunger we feel when we miss a couple of meals is really just mental habit, the reflexive desire to use food in order to regulate consciousness and control emotion. Following that reflex to its root, we find it originating from the ever-fearful ego, which is endlessly attempting to reinforce its fragile construction of a limited self inside a limited reality by keeping the mind perpetually agitated.

Of course, fasting can apply to anything physical or mental, not just what we eat. But food is fundamental. There is a natural psychic hierarchy of desires, and for most of us food is at the root of those hungers. Confronting that root hunger is also a confrontation with every other desire down the chain. This is why fasting from food is so profound for the mind, emotions, and the spirit, as well as for the physical body.

Most importantly, fasting, used carefully, with balance, and as part of a larger spiritual practice, becomes a way to help identify and unseat the despotic ego along with all of its distractions and demands.

For this reason, fasting is practiced in all religions. One doesn't even have to have religious belief, just a fearless determination to get to the heart of one's true nature.

> *Be emptier and cry like reed instruments cry.*
> *Emptier, write secrets with the reed pen.*

Clarity, insight, creativity. All of these are enhanced by fasting. We become open channels for the divine life that wants to flow through us.

Try it sometime. Fast for a day, for half a day. Wrestle your way through. See what happens.

—⁓—

Two beggars
sharing a meal of the food they've been given

The new moon shines intensely

Ko Un

English version by Brother Anthony of Taizé

Two beggars ∿

This poem does not invite us to look at these two beggars and then ask us to feed them. We are, instead, called on to see two human beings in communion, expressing their humanity even in their extremity. These two beggars are not objects of pity; they have become our teachers.

The two are hungry, yet they share the little they have with one another. They allow us to see a human connection at this quiet, desperate, yet most profound moment.

In that simple act of connection, something heavenly is recognized. And we, the witnesses, are renewed as a result, awakened from our own spiritual lethargy.

The new moon shines intensely.

—∿—

Hope says

Ithaca

When you set out on your journey to Ithaca,
pray the road is long,
filled with adventure and discovery.
The Laestrygonians and the Cyclopes,
and raging Poseidon himself, fear them not,
for you need not face them on your way
so long as your soul is uplifted, and a rare sense
stirs your spirit and quickens your body.
The Laestrygonians and the Cyclopes,
and storming Poseidon himself, you need not confront them,
so long as they do not dwell in your soul,
so long as your mind does not set them before you.

Pray the road is long.
Many will be the summer dawns
when, with what pleasure, what joy,
you will sail into ports unknown;
to stop at Phoenician markets
and buy fine things:
nacre and coral, amber and ebony,
heady spices of every kind,
as many sensual spices as you can.
To many an Egyptian city will you go
to learn, and learn more, from seekers who know.

Always do you hold Ithaca in your mind.
Arriving is your destiny.
But do not hurry the journey at all.
Better to let it last many long years
that you may set foot on the island an old man,
rich with wealth gained along the way,
expecting no treasures from Ithaca.

Ithaca has given you a wondrous journey.
Without her you'd never have set forth.
She has nothing more to give you.

And if you find her insufficient, Ithaca has not deceived you.
Wise as you'll have become, rich with experience,
you will already know what these Ithacas mean.

Constantine P. Cavafy

IMG

Ithaca ～

A little motivation to dust off that old copy of Homer's Odyssey and crack it open once again. It was a favorite of mine when I was a teenager, with its gods, monsters, heroes, adventure...

In the Odyssey, the hero Odysseus is trying to return home from the Trojan War to his island kingdom of Ithaca, but conflicts with gods and monsters and the weather keep sending him off course into new adventures. The journey takes him twenty years to finally reach his destination!

When you set out on your journey to Ithaca...

Cavafy's poem reminds us of the Odyssey's hidden truth, that the hero's journey to Ithaca is the soul's journey home.

Ancient tradition says that Homer's epics, the Iliad and the Odyssey, combine into a grand mystery tale, understood by initiates as a description of the stages and struggles of the soul's inner journey.

pray the road is long,
filled with adventure and discovery.

Too often we seekers disparage the road, its bumps and turns, impatient to reach our destination. Sometimes we never make the journey at all for fear of the gods and monsters that may stand in our way.

The Laestrygonians and the Cyclopes,
and raging Poseidon himself...

The Laestrygonians and one-eyed Cyclopes were murderous giants encountered by Odysseus on his journey, representing the terrors we imagine awaiting us along the soul's path. The one-eyed giant blinded by Odysseus and his crew turned out to be the son of Poseidon, earning them the enmity of the stormy god of the seas, and compounding their troubles on their long voyage home.

But Cavafy reassures us that we need fear neither gods nor monsters—

...fear them not,
for you need not face them on your way
so long as your soul is uplifted, and a rare sense
stirs your spirit and quickens your body.

We only ever have to confront the darkness we bring with us. We carry our own monsters. The journey is the grand stage on which we set out our demons before us so that we may confront them.

If the mind is clear and uplifted, if we do not already bear such darkness within ourselves, no monsters will rise up along the way. This does not mean no difficulties will be encountered, but the challenges hold no terror and do not bar our way.

Arriving is your destiny.

Our stops along the journey are not roadblocks, they are stepping stones. Actually, even that's not true. Seen clearly, the journey and the destination are the same. The river pours into the sea, and they are one. Resting on the slow-moving river, we already touch the sea.

There is no question that we shall arrive. The only question is what sort of journey we shall make.

But do not hurry the journey at all.

This is why we don't want to rush through the journey, impatient only for its end. When the destination is certain and only the pathway is unknown, we want to journey well, with courage and attention, for the adventure is the soul's story, reminding us that each moment is a treasure for the taking.

and buy fine things:
nacre and coral, amber and ebony,
heady spices of every kind,
as many sensual spices as you can.

Cavafy suggests that worldly experience, the senses, a certain amount of materialism, these too are part of the journey. The physical world is the realm through which the soul journeys. Encountering marvels and terrors, the soul strengthens and comes to know itself. Knowing itself in victory and adversity, the soul is finally ready to return.

36

The wisdom we attain with each step reveals the destination's true meaning.

> *Wise as you'll have become, rich with experience,*
> *you will already know what these Ithacas mean.*

And it is just as true to say that the destination's gift is the journey itself.

> *Ithaca has given you a wondrous journey.*

——∿——

Ghost Dance Songs

The whole world is coming,
a nation is coming, a nation is coming.
The Eagle has brought the message to the people.
The father says so, the father says so.
Over the whole earth they are coming.
The buffalo are coming, the buffalo are coming.
The Crow has brought the message to the people,
the father says so, the father says so.

My children, my children,
it is I who wear the morning star on my brow,
it is I who wear the morning star on my brow.
I show it to my children,
I show it to my children.

Arapaho (traditional)

English version by James Mooney

Ghost Dance Songs 〜

The buffalo are coming, the buffalo are coming.

When my wife and I first moved to Colorado, we went for long drives up in the Rocky Mountains and meandering down through the country roads spreading out from the foothills, getting to know the land. As a transplanted urbanite, the Colorado vistas were wondrous to me. One of the most startling sights was when we would come across a herd of bison or buffalo. With their massive heads, dense bodies, and mountainous shoulder humps, they seemed like prehistoric beings, earthy and primal and unsettling. I immediately loved the sight of them. We would stop by the side of the road and watch from the safety of our car. I remember one particular encounter with a bull cropping yellowed grasses close to the road. He raised his large head with the laziness of dominion and carefully eyed us before turning and rejoining his herd. A good reminder for this city kid that we, inside our car, were the aliens, while the buffalo was at home.

We imagine we are being generous when we make room for other creatures in the world, but that is a modern delusion. No matter how convinced we are that cities and human environments are the "real" world, they are all, always, built on the foundation of the natural world. Despite the enveloping reality of urban environments, human spaces are utterly dependent on the wider world of nature. We need the Earth's other creatures nearby, and in our midst, if we want a society that works within the natural world that is our only home. The more society severs that connection, the more unstable it becomes. Those strange, unsettling buffalo are essential to a human society that hopes to last.

The whole world is coming,
a nation is coming...

Toward the end of the U.S. genocidal wars against the Native American peoples in the 1800s, which were accompanied by the destruction of the great buffalo herds upon which the plains Indians depended, a visionary movement arose. At its center was the Ghost Dance, in which the spirits (or "ghosts") of the lost people and the annihilated buffalo herds were honored and summoned to return. This spiritual movement was many things in the midst of the devastation of the Native American peoples,

39

but at its core the Ghost Dance movement was a multi-tribal effort that integrated native spiritual traditions with elements of Christianity in a metaphysical effort to return the world to balance and restore what was lost. That is why these songs give us visionary affirmations, like "a nation is coming, a nation is coming" and "the buffalo are coming, the buffalo are coming."

Reading these words of invocation, it might be worth taking a few moments to contemplate not only what the native peoples of this continent have lost, but also what we all have lost, and what continues to be lost, destroyed, or pushed aside in the world today.

How do we relate to the natural world? How do we relate to the sacred? How do we relate to each other within our communities? How do we interact with other communities and other cultures? Do our social structures make room for human needs, relationships, hopes, and complexity? In other words, does society serve the world, natural and human, or merely dominate?

At the same time, we must also ask what we find that is good in modern world culture. Where does hope sprout and spirit bud? That is there too.

Is it too much to suggest that we are enacting a Ghost Dance today? We are collectively seeking a new vision for society and the world. We are struggling to reconnect with the rhythms of life and the planet in ways that give us a future. As we do so, we are discovering new reservoirs of strength and spirit.

We are engaged in a multi-cultural vision quest, but we must use awareness as we formulate our new vision. Our emerging vision has power. It may well define us for generations to come.

We must learn to ask ourselves fundamental questions about the dreams quietly running behind our daily awareness.

Every thought is an invocation. Each action is a ritual summoning. What is it that we invoke? What do we summon forth into being? What do we believe has meaning and is worth the investment of our life energies?

Do our private dreams conflict with our institutional and societal actions? And how do we respond when they do?

How do we even begin to address these questions?

A good start is for each of us to discover the life and light within, so that we may bring forth our own unique brilliance, ready to carry this flame to future generations.

> *it is I who wear the morning star on my brow.*
> *I show it to my children...*

—∿—

whatever I pick up
is alive—
ebbing tide

Chiyo-ni

English version by Gabriel Rosenstock

whatever I pick up ∿

These first two lines speak of surprise, enchantment, and the rich variety of life awaiting discovery.

> *whatever I pick up*
> *is alive—*

As a young child in Oregon, I loved visits to the coast. The Oregon coast is rocky, cold, and moody, perfect for tide pools. In my memory of those visits to the oceanside, I am little more than a toddler climbing among the rocks to discover secret tide pools, hidden pockets of water filled with colorful and strange life forms: anemones, star fish, mussels, tiny fish darting about, and the occasional hermit crab scuttling for cover. Each tide pool was a wonderland of life!

But the poem's final line—

> *ebbing tide*

—hints at death.

Chiyo-ni is right, of course. Only when the tide goes out is that magical life revealed. Yet the receding tide can feel like a personal diminishment, nature's reminder of death.

So perhaps the poem is suggesting to us that only when we recognize the reality of death is the richness of life fully revealed to us. Death challenges each of us to never take any moment of our lives for granted.

We presume death to be the loss of life and awareness and, therefore, one's self. Whatever we believe about an afterlife, death itself, when we accept its unavoidable presence, actually serves to awaken awareness and fan the fires of life within us. Death reminds us that life is not measured in years but in the fullness of our moments. The truth of death gives us permission to pause and become even more aware that whatever we pick up is alive.

—∿—

Hope says:
One day you will see her,
          if you wait well.

Says despair:
She is only your bitterness.

        Beat, my heart... Not all
        has been swallowed by the earth.

Antonio Machado

IMG

Hope says ～

We feel the heartbreak of this poem. The "her" Machado refers to is his wife, who died young. Her death is an absence that haunts many of his poems.

But this poem has a quiet courage as well. The tension between hope and despair seems impossible to resolve, but his heart makes a stand and gives that final push in favor of affirmation and life.

This poem, as a meditation on loss and grief, invites us to recognize the presence of death and perhaps consider the ways that death is a teacher. We can go so far as to say that death is our most powerful teacher. Our own death. The death of loved ones. The small daily deaths of loss and change and fear. The terrifying certainty that death eventually comes for us all.

Usually, we try not to look at death at all, at least not with a steady gaze. When forced to think about it, we are predisposed to view death as an evil, something that interrupts the way things should be. But the simple truth that death touches every aspect of existence tells us that it is essential to reality. Death is a universal presence and, therefore, a bearer of universal truth.

We must each in our own way overcome our fears and learn to learn from this indispensable teacher.

Death touches everyone, introducing us to grief and, sometimes, shattering our very sense of reality. I will not try to suggest simplistic or comfortable answers. I offer here just a few thoughts...

Death teaches us to let go. So much of life is spent in acquiring, gathering, and holding, but that becomes an imbalanced equation. Life must include letting go in order to find equilibrium. When we truly accept this, the internal act of surrender can be a great unburdening. Letting go, in great and in small ways, can be a tremendous release, like exhaling after holding one's breath.

And, when we think about it, much of spiritual practice does exactly the same thing, teaching us to let go, to exhale, allowing the unhindered rhythm of life to flow through us.

We can say that death's lesson is about non-attachment, but I would go further and say it is about non-identification. By that I mean that what truly frightens us is to let go of the things we identify with. The relationships and possessions that define our own sense of who we, those are the hardest to lose. Their loss gives us a glimpse of our own death. Some part of our self-definition is threatened by such loss, and so, psychologically, we perceive loss as a form of death.

Death, along with its milder, daily form of loss, helps us to see the many ways we have defined ourselves, the ways we have externalized ourselves, the ways we have tried to formulate a fixed idea of self. When pieces of that elaborate self-construction are removed or shifted about, we can be traumatized.

Death isn't just about physical mortality, it is the loss of identity. It is the loss of whatever we imagine ourselves to be. But, in encountering death in its lesser guises, we have the opportunity to recognize that we are still here. The foundational being that is our true self remains, regardless of what loss is experienced or how our sense of who we are has changed.

We might say that death removes the inessential to help us discover who we truly are.

Or we can say something nearly the opposite, that death takes what is absolutely essential to us in order to awaken such a pure ache that we seek for deeper meaning, a deeper understanding of reality, and a deeper sense of self.

We can say that death comes for our stories, and only takes us when we cannot let go.

Or we can say that death brings death until we discover we cannot die.

It would be foolish to argue against the all too blunt reality of physical death and the very real experience of loss in life. It is not so much that learning these lessons inoculates us against death and loss; rather, we come to understand them differently. Loss is experienced, but it is part of the eternal rhythm of life and growth. Death happens, but perhaps it is not the complete undoing of self as we feared. When we let go of our carefully constructed ideas of self and come to see the boundless, undefined being we actually are, the flow of coming and going becomes a very different experience.

> *Beat, my heart... Not all*
> *has been swallowed by the earth.*

—◆◆—

The sum total of our life is a breath
spent in the company of the Beloved.

Abu-Said Abil-Kheir

English version by Vraje Abramian

The sum total of our life ∼

I find it intriguing that "breath" and "life" and "spirit" are synonyms in many languages. When you read sacred writings and the word "spirit" is used, substitute the word "breath" and see how the meaning changes and expands.

The relationship between breath, life, and spirit is more profound than the observation that the living breathe and the dead do not.

We think in terms of borders and boundaries, constantly noting what separates ourselves, mentally and physically, from everything else. But the reality is that there is a constant flow of awareness across those borders. Every one of us has the unseen movement of the breath. Through the breath, what is outside comes inside. What is non-self becomes self. And what was self is released again out into the world. This is communion, nothing less.

That inbreath of yours is the outbreath of another. The air we breathe is the breath of all.

A deep breath opens the chest and expands the heart. A full breath requires us to feel. We feel ourselves, and we feel others. Feeling, too, is communion. When feeling is shut down, the breath is shut down, and life has become limited.

The current of the breath continuously teaches us that the boundaries of self exist only in the mental map. In reality, we flow out into the universe, and the universe flows back in. The only way to secure our borders is to stop breathing, which is, of course, death. Life requires breath, and we live in each other, within the same shared breath.

When we really breathe, we might just come to the same conclusion as the poet: An individual's lifetime may be brief or long, the experiences of life may be lasting or fleeting, but this communal breath-life-spirit in which we participate is the very breath of the Beloved.

—∿—

Whoever finds love
beneath hurt and grief
disappears into emptiness
with a thousand new disguises

Rumi

English version by Coleman Barks

Whoever finds love ✑

Whoever finds love
beneath hurt and grief
disappears into emptiness
with a thousand new disguises

We live our lives, most of us, with a nearly imperceptible veil draped across everything. This dusty gossamer acts as a filter, slightly obscuring and coloring everything we perceive or imagine. That veil is intimately interwoven with the ego. When the veil falls away we too "disappear." That is, the isolated ego-self we imagined ourselves to be vanishes. The mind grows quiet. The false self disappears. And we see the world as it is.

The world of disconnected beings and objects, the world we have spent a lifetime assuming to be unassailable reality, dissolves before our eyes. We are left, instead, with a unified wholeness that is dynamic and alive, but no longer populated by separated selves and things. We can call this emptiness.

Like the rest of reality, we have become fluid and formless. In this sense, we are spaciousness within unlimited space. This is how the mystic "disappears into emptiness."

Being without form, we still assume a form to participate in the realm of form. What was once the trap of a fixed identity becomes a game. We pretend to be someone, so other someones can relate to us. We wear masks that suit the situation, and then change them as the situation changes. Yet those masks are not who we are in any absolute sense, and we know this. Being formless, we can assume any form. As Rumi says, we gain "a thousand new disguises."

But it is the beginning phrase that I keep rereading:

Whoever finds love
beneath hurt and grief...

We are predisposed to use hurt and grief, loss and pain, as a barrier. We reflexively tense in order to numb the pain we feel. That is natural. The problem is that we all accumulate griefs in life and become far too adept at anticipating hurts, so we live in a continual state of tension and partial numbness. The result is that we do not fully participate in the living moment, which is the dwelling place of life and joy.

Rumi's words remind us to muster the courage necessary to dive beneath the hurt and the grief and not fear them. For the aspect of the mind that is entirely concerned with self-preservation and comfort, there is a certain blasphemy to even imagine something healing and joyful—"love"—beneath the surface of our pains. But it is just that sort of blasphemy, that sacred disregard for psychic comfort, that leads us to the most startling experience of love.

These lines give us permission to stop waiting for some future when pain is past. What we seek is found right here, patiently waiting for us to dig just a bit deeper.

—◊◊—

The dazzling darkness

Lead us up beyond light,
beyond knowing and unknowing,
to the topmost summit of truth,

where the mysteries lie hidden,
unchanging and absolute,
in the dazzling darkness
of the secret silence.
All light is outshined
by the intensity of their shade.

The senses are flooded, the mind made blind
by such unseen beauty
beyond all beauty.

Dionysius the Areopagite

IMG

Lead us up beyond light ᔍ

Although this poem may be unfamiliar, it is immensely important to the history of Western mysticism and spirituality. Virtually all European esoteric traditions have drawn inspiration and meaning from it, directly or indirectly. I invite you to take a moment to reread its lines and consider why it has inspired centuries of spiritual seekers.

Dionysius is telling us something about knowledge and the limitations of knowledge, using the metaphor of light and darkness.

> *Lead us up beyond light,*
> *beyond knowing and unknowing,*
> *to the topmost summit of truth...*

We might say that intellectual knowledge is knowledge dependent on the visible, things in the light. But clearly Dionysius feels that such knowledge does not attain the "topmost summit of truth."

There is another level of knowing, deeper, more obscure, yet all-encompassing. This is the knowledge sought by the mystic. This is the knowledge found in utter silence that connects us with genuine truth.

Amidst this darkness, the truth shines.

> *...where the mysteries lie hidden,*
> *unchanging and absolute,*
> *in the dazzling darkness*
> *of the secret silence.*

That mystifying phrase about the "dazzling darkness," like a Christian koan, has been contemplated endlessly and keeps reappearing in esoteric writings. It sounds like a spiritual word game, but the poet is actually describing something very specific.

In profound communion, seeing in the normal sense stops. It is not that perception on the mundane level ceases (except, perhaps, in the most ecstatic states), but surfaces take on a thin or unreal quality. Everything that formerly seemed so real and tangible has become ghost-like, more of a concept than a fixed reality. Surfaces and categories—the foundation of mundane perception—become ephemeral, dreamlike, insubstantial.

Nothing is left. That is, because there is no longer a sense of separation, the reality of distinct objects dims. Instead, what we perceive is an underlying fluidity of being that runs through everything and everyone, rendering the idea of separate beings and objects absurd.

It is as if the visible world is actually a world of shadow, while underlying that is a realm of brilliance and interwoven beauty.

The senses are flooded, the mind made blind
by such unseen beauty
beyond all beauty.

The surface world, which once filled our senses, has been eclipsed, and all we now see is the innate radiance of existence—the dazzling darkness.

—◦◦◦—

I Entered the Unknown

I entered the unknown,
and there I remained unknowing,
all knowledge transcended.

Where I entered I knew not,
but seeing myself there,
not knowing where,
great things then made themselves known.
What I sensed I cannot say,
for I remained unknowing,
all knowledge transcended.

In this peace and purity
was perfect knowledge.
In profoundest solitude
I understood with absolute clarity
something so secret
that I was left stammering,
all knowledge transcended.

So deep was I within,
so absorbed, transported,
that all senses fled,
and outer awareness fell away.
My spirit received the gift
of unknowing knowing,
all knowledge transcended.

He who reaches this realm
loses himself,
for all he once knew
now is beneath his notice,
and his mind so expands
that he remains unknowing,
all knowledge transcended.

And the higher he rises
the less he knows:
That is the dark cloud
that shines in the night.
The one who knows this
always remains unknowing,
all knowledge transcended.

This knowing by unknowing
is of such exalted power,
that the disputations of the learned
fail to grasp it,
for their knowledge does not reach
to knowing by unknowing,
all knowledge transcended.

Of such supreme perfection
is this knowledge
that no faculty or method of mind
can comprehend it;
but he who conquers himself
with this unknowing knowing,
will always transcend.

And if you are ready to receive it,
this sum of all knowledge is discovered
in the deepest ecstasy
of the Divine Essence.
Goodness and grace
grant us this unknowing,
all knowledge transcended.

John of the Cross

IMG

I Entered the Unknown ∼℧

St. John of the Cross repeatedly contrasts knowledge with
unknowing.

> *I entered the unknown,*
> *and there I remained unknowing,*
> all knowledge transcended.

The Spanish word rendered here as "knowledge" is *ciencia*, which
has the more obvious translation of "science." But the poem's
archaic use of "science" implies not the scientific process, but a
more general sense of knowledge acquired through reason and the
testimony of the senses.

And John of the Cross emphasizes that his unknowing is superior.

He is not advocating ignorance, however. The Spanish saint is
instead speaking about the mystical idea of "unknowing," the
state in which all concepts and mental filters have been set aside.
In that state of unknowing, we rise above the elaborate
constructions of the logical mind and come to rest in pure
awareness ("knowing by unknowing"). He is contrasting true,
unfiltered knowing, gnosis, with the mere accumulation and
organization of information.

To be unknowing in this sense is to encounter every instant
entirely as it is, in pure wonder, without projection, without
anticipation or agitation. The intellectual mind—a hugely
important tool!—has one very serious weakness: It never
encounters the present moment nakedly. It is always processing,
analyzing, making everything fit within its comprehension. It
never truly witnesses; it only interprets.

We certainly want to cultivate a critical intellect, but we must
always remember that it is not the whole of consciousness. The
awareness can step beyond the intellect. To fully apprehend
reality, it must.

> *So deep was I within,*
> *so absorbed, transported,*
> *that all senses fled,*
> *and outer awareness fell away.*

This state of supreme unknowing is not perception in the sense of drawing in and interpreting exterior input through the senses. In normal perception, the intellect sifts and sorts that sensory data and formulates it into a working hypothesis of what reality is. That hypothesis, however, is always an incomplete shorthand that only approximates reality.

By contrast, the mystic's unknowing is the centered awareness of unfiltered reality. This awareness does not tilt off its seat in order to reach out through the senses. It is at rest, poised. It witnesses without an egoic agenda. The full awareness in this state of unknowing does not sift reality, it bathes in it.

Rather than an interpretation, one sees clearly, free from artificial mental constructions—knowing by unknowing.

> *And if you are ready to hear it,*
> *this sum of all knowledge is discovered*
> *in the deepest ecstasy*
> *of the Divine Essence.*
> *Goodness and grace*
> *grant us this unknowing,*
> all knowledge transcended.

This transcendence of knowledge, which is simultaneously the "sum of all knowledge" is found to be an experience of "the deepest ecstasy / of the Divine Essence." This is the "goodness and grace" found by the mind as it basks in unfiltered awareness.

—⁓—

Among mountain caves,
Within the forest's shade,
Inside a hut set in green fields,
Or beneath canopies of white cotton—

The yogi is free,
    everywhere his home.

Shabkar

IMG

Among mountain caves ～

Among mountain caves,
Within the forest's shade...

The idea of retreating into the desert or the forest always had a romantic appeal to me, especially as a young man.

Thoreau's *Walden* was a close companion, and I regularly reread his lines on living the essential life:

> *I went to the woods because I wished to live deliberately, to front only the essential facts of life, and see if I could not learn what it had to teach, and not, when I came to die, discover that I had not lived. I did not wish to live what was not life, living is so dear; nor did I wish to practise resignation, unless it was quite necessary. I wanted to live deep and suck out all the marrow of life, to live so sturdily and Spartan-like as to put to rout all that was not life...*

Such a person experiences an intense need to silence the mind, to settle the heart, and to sweep life clean of everything unnecessary in order to feel the pulse that proves the living presence beneath the skin of existence.

To accomplish this, like Shabkar's yogi, we want to retreat from the world. But what do we mean by "the world"? We can loosely say that it is society, but that is too simplistic. The world we are trying to withdraw from is more of an idea of reality. By withdrawing, we are attempting to separate from the consensus trance.

We forget that even in our most pragmatic, mundane activity, we are in trance. We don't enter trance only in those rarified moments, like the yogi in his ecstasy. We are always in trance. And we are always seeking trance. We humans are trance-seeking creatures. Virtually every choice we make is about cultivating trance. We watch TV and surf the Internet because of the trance it induces. We eat food for how it makes us feel as much as for nourishment. Falling in love is trance. Family conversation around the dinner table is trance. A good day at work is one form of trance, and a bad day is another trance. Every action of every day is an attempt to fine-tune our mental and emotional states because of how they affect our perception of reality. We are endlessly forming and reforming trance.

The problem is that early in life we come to believe that a very limited range of trance is the full spectrum of reality. We all subscribe to this in order to be acceptable and considered "normal" within society. As children moving into adolescence, taking on that consensus trance is important. It allows us to stabilize psychologically and form healthy relationships with others. It is also a serious problem, since it has nothing to do with actual limitations of reality or our true nature.

It is this shared trance that we call the world, which seekers instinctively withdraw from in order to see truly, free from the psychic pressures of society to remain within its limited bandwidth of awareness. When done with balance, steadiness, and reverence, such withdrawal from the common bubble of presumed reality can lead to surprising clarity, opening, and bliss.

But there is a potential spiritual pitfall in the idea of retreat from the world as well. Retreat necessarily implies separation. In withdrawing from the world, we are separating from what we imagine to be blind and lost humanity. In the struggle to free oneself from the gravitational pull of consensus reality, it is possible to become rigid, disdainful, even hard-hearted. We have divided reality between what is sacred or true from the mundane and illusory. Such a division, any division, within our view of reality can never hold up, for it does not admit the vision of the undivided Whole.

Here is how I understand the solution to this dilemma: That instinct to separate oneself in order to discover an awareness that is pure and essential—whether through literal retreat or some form of internal solitude—can be enormously helpful along the spiritual journey. But, for most of us, it is a phase of the journey and not the end goal. We may choose to disappear into the desert, to climb into a mountain cave, or perhaps just create a hidden corner amidst urban life, but we must still remain connected to the world through compassion and commitment. And that connection may well call upon us to return to the world to live and act and be present within it, while no longer feeling trapped by its gravitational pull and artificial boundaries.

We come to recognize that the constricted space we knew as "the world" is not separate from the wider reality or in opposition to it.

The Eternal is present in it all. And so are we. It is all home. Everywhere is home.

> *The yogi is free,*
> *everywhere his home.*

———∿∿∿———

But leave the Wise to wrangle

In my hut
mice and fireflies
getting along

Issa

English version by Gabriel Rosenstock

in my hut ～

Several of Issa's poems evoke fireflies. They seem to represent a luminous aspect of the awareness, that which hovers with quiet delight in the summer evening—elevated and illuminated, wondrous, perhaps fleeting.

I imagine Issa's mice to be the thoughts of the busy mind. They scurry and scratch, dig into everything, pausing now and then to squeak from hidden corners.

So, do your mice and fireflies get along?

—〰—

So I say: Mind, don't you sleep
Or Time is going to get in and steal from you.

You hold on to the sword of Kali's name.
The shield of Tara's name.

Can Death overwhelm you?
Sound Kali's name on a horn and sound it loud.

Chant "Durga, Durga,"
Until you bring the dawn around.

If She won't save you in this Dark Age—.
But how many great sinners have been saved!

Is Ramprasad then
So unsalvageable a rogue?

Ramprasad

English version by Leonard Nathan and Clinton Seely

Mind, don't you sleep ⁓

Ramprasad's songs to the Mother Goddess Kali were like dynamite to my early seeking. I discovered his poetry while reading about the 19th century Hindu saint, Ramakrishna, who, in ecstatic states, would recite the poetry of Ramprasad.

> *So I say: Mind, don't you sleep*

Most of us think we are the mind. But here the poet speaks to the mind as a separate entity. He creates a parental relationship with the mind, protective and also chiding.

This is actually an effective technique. When the mind wants to scatter, if we assume that we are the mind, then what can we do? But when we recognize the mind as a flow of consciousness under our care, then we can influence it to correct its disruptive tendencies, training it to remain alert and still—"Mind, don't you sleep."

> *Or Time is going to get in and steal from you.*

There is a play of meanings in this poem: The Great Goddess manifests through the cycles of becoming and dissolution... and, thus, she is associated with time. Time is Kali's game of apparent change. The root word for time is *kal.* Kali overcomes *kal.* When we are awake, we consciously participate in Kali's game of time rather than become lost within it.

> *You hold on to the sword of Kali's name.*
> *The shield of Tara's name.*

Here Ramprasad is making a distinction between the Mother Goddess as Kali and as Tara. Kali is the Goddess in her terrifying aspect, she who ecstatically cuts through delusion. For this reason, Kali carries a sword.

Tara, on the other hand, is the protective aspect of the Divine Mother, so Tara's name is a shield.

Time and death are paired in this poem as the ultimate limitations on life that must be transcended in order to experience the eternal nature of being. But how does one transcend what seem to be inescapable aspects of reality?

Chant "Durga, Durga,"

Ramprasad's prescription is to chant the divine name. But what does chanting have to do with time or death?

The practice of chanting, done with attention, brings the mind to a focused stillness. As this deepens, one's relationship with time shifts. In mundane awareness, we take time for granted as the inevitable unfolding of serial events. But time reveals itself as something different to the quiet awareness. Events still occur, but we stop inserting our own self-importance into their midst. Instead of tumbling helplessly with the current of events through time, it is as if we have found our footing and stand still to witness the flow all around us. Movement occurs, but the personal sense of time stops.

And here's the thing about death: In states of ecstatic awareness, the mystic is flooded with an unimpeded sense of life. By comparison, all other experiences seem as if they belong to the realm of sleep. There is the sense that the common experience of life is somehow encrusted with a layer of—let's call it death—that has dampened the full awareness of life. In this newly vivified state, death has left us. Only life remains. This doesn't mean that the physical body won't eventually grow old and cease to function. But life's experiences lose the bitter flavor of death.

Until you bring the dawn around.

The moment when one awakens from that long sleep is also accompanied by a dazzling flood of light—"the dawn."

Such levels of spiritual awakening may sound like something attainable only through unimaginable effort by only the most perfect masters, but that thought, while masquerading as humility, becomes an excuse used by the mind to allow it to remain asleep.

Ramprasad laughs as he short circuits that lethargic psychic reflex.

Is Ramprasad then
So unsalvageable a rogue?

Look at the strange lot of people who have stumbled their way to enlightenment. By comparison, is any one of us "so unsalvageable a rogue?" There is a saying that a saint is a sinner who never gave up. Rogues too realize.

Come

Every day I am astonished by
how little I know, and discouraged,
obedient as I am to the demand to
know more—always more.

But then there is the slow seep
of light from the day,
and I look to the west where
the hills are darkening,

setting their shoulders to the night,
and the sky peppered with pillows
of mist, their bellies burnt
by the furnace of the sun.

And it is then that I notice
the invitation didn't say, *Come
armed with knowledge and a loud voice.*
It only said, *Come.*

Andrew Colliver

Come ∽

Every day I am astonished by
how little I know, and discouraged,
obedient as I am to the demand to
know more—always more.

Reading these lines makes me smile. It is as if some part of my
own self is speaking to me through them.

Like so many self-described seekers, I was born with a hungry
head. I always wanted to *know*. I was curious about everything,
how things work, how things connect, why things are the way
they are. So, naturally, I approached the spiritual journey the
same way.

The strength in such a method is that it encourages us to bring
our full focus to our spirituality. The questioning mind, the
curious mind, the cynical mind, the discriminating mind—these
can be powerful allies, drawing together one's energies, focusing
them toward a goal, allowing us to continuously examine and
reformulate our sense of self and our understanding of reality.

That's the good aspect. The problem is that this mental
discrimination can imprison us within the head. One can easily
fall into the trap of turning the spiritual journey into an
intellectual enterprise, confusing the acquisition of spiritual
information with genuine awareness.

As I came to terms with this tendency in myself, I found a hidden
neurosis at work: On some level, I held the idea that I must
somehow earn spiritual depth. In my personal makeup, the way I
tried to prove my worthiness was through building a fortress of
knowledge.

That basic thought of not being worthy without the proof of
impressive knowledge became a barrier to my own process of
opening. The more spiritual information I acquired, whether from
books or teachers or even though my own direct experience,
reinforced that primary barrier. I was polishing the ego,
reaffirming it, even as I was trying to be more "spiritual."

When so much of one's proposed future enlightenment is built on
the idea of accumulated spiritual knowledge, trying to move

beyond that hoard of well-organized mental treasures can feel like stepping out into snow blindness. It can seem like the loss of all landmarks in the midst of a daunting journey.

Humility and trust become necessary to walk an unknown path. We must be willing to get lost, to look like a fool, and to disappoint our peers. Bruised and disoriented, we learn to feel our way. Feeling, we begin to discover the heart and its secret intelligence.

Rational thought and spiritual study can provide us with a much-needed map along with the internal tools to assess the landscape. But the job is not to paper the walls of our meditation rooms with maps. We must actually make the journey, feeling each step of land beneath our feet. Whether we bring one map or a stack of atlases or walk with empty hands, it is unknown territory we step into. We are travelers amidst great mystery.

Best not to worry overmuch about knowledge or earning our way. We are all already worthy. Knowing that, we know enough. All that remains is to answer the call and give ourselves permission to take that first step. And then keep going.

> *And it is then that I notice*
> *the invitation didn't say,* Come
> armed with knowledge and a loud voice.
> *It only said,* Come.

But leave the Wise to wrangle, and with me
The Quarrel of the Universe let be:
    And, in some corner of the Hubbub couch'd,
Make Game of that which makes as much of Thee.

Omar Khayyam

English version by Edward FitzGerald

But leave the Wise to wrangle ∿

But leave the Wise to wrangle, and with me
The Quarrel of the Universe let be:

The keepers of religion love theological debates, displaying their
command of what others have said about the nature of God and
reality. Khayyam, like most mystics, has little patience for their
endless squabbles. Ceaselessly circling duels of wit and scriptural
citation belong to the realm of self-importance and intellect. They
do not lead to inner awareness. A true seeker is only satisfied
with direct perception. Theory and debate can never satisfy the
seeking heart.

And, in some corner of the Hubbub couch'd...

Khayyam urges us instead to find a quiet spot outside the bustle
in order seek truth without distraction.

Make Game of that which makes as much of Thee.

While everyone else is jostling to be acknowledged for their
superior rhetoric and scriptural knowledge, Khayyam invites us
into a game. This is no ordinary game, however. It is the game of
God, the only game truly worth playing.

God makes game of us all, obviously. Call it fate or karma, the
great currents of life and history, the particulars of family and
society, the material world's countless stage props thrust in our
way. Most of us recognize only this aspect of the game, a reality
that acts upon us. We may bring some measure of will and
creativity in order to rearrange those pieces and slightly redirect
their momentum. But that is a losing strategy because it is
playing against the board, not the player.

Only the lovers of God are truly engaged enough to play a two-
way game. They understand that the purpose is not to win or lose.
The game is just an excuse to enjoy the company of the Friend.

—∿—

When all is finally seen as it is,
    nothing hidden behind the fantasies of the mind—
That is Tathagata.
That alone is the state of compassionate knowledge.
Once this is realized, karma and its obstacles
    disappear into emptiness.
But until that moment,
    one's debts must be paid.

Yoka Genkaku

IMG

When all is finally seen as it is ∽

> *When all is finally seen as it is,*
>   *nothing hidden behind the fantasies of the mind—*
> *That is Tathagata.*

The term Tathagata is a name given to the Buddha that can be translated as "one who stands upon what is, one who resides in unmodified reality." The implication is that one must perceive reality as it is, not through the imperfect filters of the mundane mind. The normal mind has trouble seeing clearly because it tends to project meaning and ideas onto all it perceives. The mind sees its thoughts about reality, not reality itself. For most of us, full reality remains "hidden behind the fantasies of the mind."

To attain the clarity of true knowledge and a genuine relationship with reality, we must drop our mental filters in order to perceive directly.

> *That alone is the state of compassionate knowledge.*

I find the closing lines on karma to be especially interesting—

> *Once this is realized, karma and its obstacles*
>   *disappear into emptiness.*
> *But until that moment,*
>   *one's debts must be paid.*

There are a few ways we can understand the working of karma. On a rather basic level, we might think of karma as positive or negative marks on our spiritual accounting ledger. We imagine two columns, our karmic debts on one side and what I have heard humorously referred to as "virtue points" on the other. All of our bad actions and thoughts must eventually be balanced out with the good. We don't want to end up in the red!

The monotheistic religions have similar ideas of sin balanced by love and charitable works.

These notions of spiritual debts, when utilized properly, can encourage greater humility, self-reflection, and the cultivation of a compassionate heart.

But there are more esoteric ways to understand karma. The word "karma" literally means "action," and in its most obvious form it is just that—action and reaction. But, from a spiritual point of view, karma is specifically *compelled* action, inevitably paired with its results as they manifest through time.

Karma is powered by an unconscious urge to think and choose and act within certain patterns. When we express that compelled karma in our lives, we reinforce the pattern, increasing the impulse to repeat it again in the future. This is the wheel of karma. It sounds a lot like addiction, doesn't it?

Karmic activity always involves effort, ego, and subtly compromised will, along with repetition through habitual cycles.

When we investigate these patterns, we see that underlying our karmic actions are points of tension in the awareness. These act as knots in one's psyche and trap a great deal of our life energy. Our psychic tensions compel certain behaviors and mental fixations while attracting associated experiences.

But, through compassionate action used as a counter-balance, those karmic knots can be loosened and finally released. Understood this way, positive karmic action is not really about clearing out bad karma or sins, it becomes more of a process of energetic mastery, reintegration, and self-liberation.

Yet this is still dealing with karma as action and reaction in order to reconcile one's debts.

There is another level beyond the making of deposits and withdrawals in one's spiritual bank account, beyond even untangling those energetic hindrances one-by-one. At a certain point, karma itself is revealed to be empty and without further compulsion.

There is a state in which all karma-inducing tensions just fall away. The entire awareness, free from its projections and attachments, suddenly relaxes out of its knots all at once, like shrugging off a heavy overcoat on a hot day.

When the psychic knots fade, karmic action ceases. Activity may continue, but it is actionless action, with no sense of self or compulsion. Events still occur, sometimes difficult ones, but it is no longer felt as a weight on one's being. One simply experiences the flow of life.

This is how some adepts can boldly claim that they are free from karma or that it has become empty for them.

But to hear someone state that karma is fundamentally empty does not mean we can ignore its functioning within our own lives. So long as the karmic burden is still felt, then the proper work is to lighten its load through compassionate action and spiritual practice—"But until that moment, / one's debts must be paid." This is the work that slowly loosens the garment until, in one liberating moment, it falls away. It is then that we see it was weightless all along!

I think of these two levels of working with karma as having parallels with the Christian notions of the Law of Justice and the Law of Love. The normal working of karma, that is, action leading to reaction leading to more action, with payment required for every debt, is the Law of Justice. It is spiritually important, but it can also become an endless cycle. Through the Law of Love, however, we transcend the Law of Justice. When one attains a state of clarity, selflessness, and profound compassion, the hard mathematics of karma is replaced with the unbound artistry of one's full being.

—◦◦◦—

Trippers and askers surround me,
People I meet, the effect upon me of my early life or the ward
    and city I live in, or the nation,
The latest dates, discoveries, inventions, societies, authors old and
    new,
My dinner, dress, associates, looks, compliments, dues,
The real or fancied indifference of some man or woman I love,
The sickness of one of my folks or of myself, or ill-doing or loss
    or lack of money, or depressions or exaltations,
Battles, the horrors of fratricidal war, the fever of doubtful news,
    the fitful events;
These come to me days and nights and go from me again,
But they are not the Me myself.
Apart from the pulling and hauling stands what I am,
Stands amused, complacent, compassionating, idle, unitary,
Looks down, is erect, or bends an arm on an impalpable certain
    rest,
Looking with side-curved head curious what will come next,
Both in and out of the game and watching and wondering at it.
Backward I see in my own days where I sweated through fog with
    linguists and contenders,
I have no mockings or arguments, I witness and wait.

Walt Whitman

Trippers and askers surround me ∿

Trippers and askers surround me...

People, society, busyness, news, work, position, love, health, emotion, terror, elation—the world. So much surrounds us and swirls about, crying constantly for attention. We get caught up in the drama and pageantry, all our suffering and our victories. We derive our sense of value and well-being according to their ebb and flow.

Yet all this is what we experience, not what we are.

But they are not the Me myself.

This is more than a reassuring idea to help us mentally regroup. We can arrive at a point where we no longer feel the gravitational tug of it all. The "pulling and hauling" may not stop, yet we find ourselves seated in easy majesty amidst of the maelstrom. Surrounded by activity, engaged in activity, the real "Me" remains at rest, invulnerable, whole, clear-seeing.

Apart from the pulling and hauling stands what I am,
Stands amused, complacent, compassionating, idle, unitary,
Looks down, is erect, or bends an arm on an impalpable certain rest...

Whitman gives us this evocative image of the "unitary" self as it "bends an arm on an impalpable certain rest." Without obvious or tangible support, this inner self nonetheless rests in steady equanimity.

While so much action and emotion circle about us, what does this self in its unity do? It sees. It "witnesses."

Looking with side-curved head curious what will come next,
Both in and out of the game and watching and wondering at it...

It does not judge. It does not even isolate or categorize specific experiences. This self sees all at once, as a living whole.

I have no mockings or arguments, I witness and wait.

Seeing this way, the self knows. It knows interrelationships and patterns, the indivisibility of things. Through this vision, nothing

82

is separate. Any single thread's tension pulls all the way through the tapestry.

In recognizing a universe in which everything lives and exists within everything else, compassion becomes the natural attitude toward all things. We become "compassionating."

This integrated vision is what the universe seeks through us. Our purpose is fulfilled in acting as the eyes through which the universe knows itself once more.

—⁓—

Neither color nor form

The mind
    is a reflection in the mirror:
    there, yet not there.

When the mind is at rest,
    the world too is at peace.

Grasping neither existence nor emptiness,
you are neither wise nor holy,
just a simple man who has completed his work.

Layman P'ang

IMG

The mind is a reflection in the mirror ～

When the mind is at rest,
  the world too is at peace.

We imagine that if the world would just settle down for a
moment, then perhaps we could experience peace. And so we turn
all of our efforts outward, trying to force a sense of order upon the
world. Of course, that doesn't work so well.

Yet, if we instead turn inward, that can feel like a betrayal, as if
we have abandoned the outer world to chaos, while we seek a
selfish peace.

Contrary to those instincts, we don't create a peaceful
environment and then experience peace. The reality is the
reverse. We discover peace within, and only then can we recognize
it without. More surprising still is that we come to see that the
world outside of ourselves is but a reflection of our own inner
state. When we recognize peace within, the world comes to rest as
well.

Does this mean that troubles in the world disappear? No. But we
recognize that there is, for no obvious external reason, a radiant
peace underneath even the worst problems. Seeing that, we begin
to see new ways to coax that peace to the surface.

At peace, in peace, we become better at creating peace.

Grasping neither existence nor emptiness...

The tool of the thinking mind is exceptionally useful for
categorizing and dividing reality, but even at its most subtle and
incisive, it is incapable of witnessing the holistic vision that
invites us to bathe in reality without grasping at it.

When the mind is truly at peace, not only have thoughts come to
rest, but, more importantly, those unconscious psychic filters
drop, and we no longer pre-sift our perception of reality.

Layman P'ang gives a trail for us to follow, a path found precisely
where existence meets emptiness, and we must gracefully walk
between the two. Clinging to neither manifestation nor void, we

witness the whole of reality at rest. When one simply is, all of reality naturally is, as well, and peace is discovered.

Enfolded in this truth, we are not wise or holy—those are further categories. We just are.

...just a simple man who has completed his work.

We no longer feel the need to do something to validate our existence. Beyond all definition, we are.

No work remains to be done. One may still be active, but there is no effort behind it, just the dance of presence and flow.

All the stories we once repeated to prop up the little self have fallen silent. We become unremarkable, purely as we are— ordinary in this extraordinary world.

—∿—

The mind has neither color nor form.
Search for it: it is nowhere.
Emptiness!

Shabkar

English version by Matthieu Ricard

The mind has neither color nor form ~

Something in human instinct recoils from statements like, "The mind... is nowhere." This fear is a natural reflex of psychic self-preservation. Consciously or unconsciously we assume that we are the mind. So to say that the mind is nowhere feels as if we are marching headlong into self-negation.

It can be highly entertaining to watch our mental contortions trying to accept this notion while still rejecting it in our gut. The mind can perform amazing acrobatics imagining its own non-existence!

Here's one way to understand this oft repeated teaching of no mind: The mind must begin the search, but it cannot complete it. At a certain point, what we call the mind is recognized as a hindrance to full, clear perception. There usually follows a long process of trying to figure out how to sidestep the mind. This leads only to limited success as we begin to comprehend that we are, in fact, not the mind. Yet even when we reluctantly acknowledge this truth to ourselves, we have no real idea how to get around the limitations of the mind.

Eventually we ask more fundamental questions, like what is the mind? We begin to watch it, observing its thoughts and images, its habits and attachments, its likes and dislikes, and ask, is this me? One fleeting thought, followed by another thought, and then another, are they somehow what I am? What part of me feels this feeling I am feeling? The image hovering in my awareness, did I conjure it? I see a thing and then I form a mental image of the thing and then I think about the mental image I have formed. Do I ever really see a thing as it is? This flow of thought, perception, and thought about perception, what is it all really? How am I mind and how am I that which observes the mind?

This is not meant to be a heady, intellectual process. We don't necessarily need to formulate these questions into words at all. We just watch. Through watching, we grow quiet. Through watching, we learn to see.

A curious thing begins to happen: We become more stable, while the mind dissipates. It is not even really that the mind fades. The mind's reality fades. We begin to see that the mind is not a sustained thing at all. It has no existence in and of itself. It is

89

found to be like ripples upon the surface of a running stream, simply the result of movement. When the movement stops, the water remains, but the ripples are gone.

Awareness remains. "I" remain. But thoughts cease and mind settles into spacious emptiness. And there we stand finally witnessing ourselves and all that is, without the intervening disruption of thoughts about our thoughts about our thoughts.

Rather than a universe filled with an endless catalog of objects and experiences, there is but a single radiance. Because this profound sense of integration is free from the idea of separate, objectified "things," there is nothing there. There are no "things." We can therefore call it Emptiness. But the life and the beauty we find is so abundant that we would never make the mistake of describing it as a negation. It is a summation. It is a reunification of awareness within the totality of Being.

That impish mind, search for it. Laugh at its escapes and evasions. We cannot find the mind. But we find so much more.

—◊—

Vanity of Spirit

Quite spent with thoughts, I left my cell, and lay
Where a shrill spring tun'd to the early day.
    I begg'd here long, and groan'd to know
    Who gave the clouds so brave a bow,
    Who bent the spheres, and circled in
    Corruption with this glorious ring;
    What is His name, and how I might
    Descry some part of His great light.

I summon'd Nature; pierc'd through all her store;
Broke up some seals, which none had touch'd before
    Her womb, her bosom, and her head,
    Where all her secrets lay abed,
    I rifled quite; and having past
    Through all the creatures, came at last
    To search my self, where I did find
    Traces, and sounds of a strange kind.

Here of this mighty spring I found some drills,
With echoes beaten from th' eternal hills.
    Weak beams and fires flash'd to my sight,
    Like a young East, or moonshine night,
    Which show'd me in a nook cast by
    A piece of much antiquity,
    With hieroglyphics quite dismember'd,
    And broken letters scarce remember'd.

I took them up, and—much joy'd—went about
T' unite those pieces, hoping to find out
    The mystery; but this ne'er done,
    That little light I had was gone.
    It griev'd me much. At last, said I,
    "Since in these veils my eclips'd eye
    May not approach Thee—for at night
    Who can have commerce with the light?—
    I'll disapparel, and to buy
    But one half-glance, most gladly die."

Henry Vaughan

Vanity of the Spirit 〜

One important detail from the life of Henry Vaughan to help us
unlock this poem: His brother, Thomas Vaughan, was a famous
Hermetic philosopher and alchemist of the English Renaissance.
The ideas of alchemy and Hermeticism were circulating among
the intellectual, artistic, and spiritual communities at the time.
Henry Vaughan, like his brother, was clearly immersed in this
esoteric language and spirituality, which combined Hermetic
mysticism with rapidly evolving British ideas of Christianity.

This entire poem is an alchemical meditation on spiritual
awakening.

Vaughan begins with the alchemical notion that one must
discover the secrets held by the natural world, secrets protected
by mystical seals:

> *I summon'd Nature; pierc'd through all her store;*
> *Broke up some seals, which none had touch'd before...*

But, after seeing into the essence of natural forces, he recognizes
that the most important secret is contained within himself: "...and
having past / Through all the creatures, came at last / To search
my self..."

Searching within, Vaughan discovers a state of awareness
described by mystics throughout the world. He experiences a
sensation of water bubbling up within ("this mighty spring") and
a soft, reverberating tone he evocatively describes as "echoes
beaten from th' eternal hills." He also witnesses an ineffable light
that is like a soft dawn or moonlight:

> *Weak beams and fires flash'd to my sight,*
> *Like a young East, or moonshine night.*

Basking in this light, his awareness expands, revealing scattered
truths, showing him "...hieroglyphics quite dismember'd, / And
broken letters scarce remember'd."

He also expresses the natural philosopher's instinct to gather the
results of the alchemical Work and join them together:

I took them up, and—much joy'd—went about
T' unite those pieces, hoping to find out
The mystery...

These disparate "pieces" are, in truth, fragments of the individual's awareness, and it is the job of the Hermetic philosopher to refine them and draw them together into conjunction, which is also union with the Divine. But he admits that this task was "ne'er done," and soon his elevated perception dissipates. The "veils" once more "eclipse" his eyes.

Does he eventually succeed? Is he once again filled with the light? Does he rediscover the upwelling spring or the sound echoing off the hills? The poem does not tell us. But I suspect the answer is yes, because he clearly recognizes the final ingredient necessary to complete his alchemical Work: surrender of the self. In the final two lines he decides to become utterly naked ("I'll disapparel") and drop the ego ("to buy / But one half-glance, most gladly die.").

This is the key to the alchemical formula.

—∿—

words do not come
there is no need for profound utterances or
deep truths
here is an ordinary evening
why spoil it with dramatic overstatement

the silence amidst the noise
the gem at the core
of every experience
is polished by simple attention
into shining magnificence

Nirmala

Words do not come ∿

We want our lives to be grand, important. We want our existence to feel *significant*. The more spiritually focused we are, the more we want everything our mind encounters to be profound. That instinct at first helps us out of our inertia, but it eventually becomes one more way for the self-important self to reinforce itself.

The goal is not profound thoughts or grand experiences. We don't need to become significant. We *are* significant. We just need to experience the moment honestly, clearly, without self-projection. It is then that the mundane moment is truly seen for the first time. Polished by our own attention, the moment shines with a light that is hidden to the superficial glance.

We do not need to make something happen in the world or in ourselves. All we need do is let the moment shine.

—∿—

The temple bell dies away.
The scent of flowers in the evening
Is still tolling the bell.

Basho

English version by R. H. Blyth

The temple bell dies away ～

Twilight in springtime, with evening descending. We sit with
Basho on his porch beneath the eaves of his house.

The temple bell itself has already rung and fallen silent. We hear
its sustained reverberation as the echo fades into the failing light.

With eyelids half closed, we breathe in the evening air and catch
the honeyed scent of spring blossoms. Another breath, slow and
deep, in through the nose. Hold it for a heartbeat to taste the
sweetness on the air. A delicate moment, suspended and timeless.
Then an easy exhale.

As the temple bell fades, a new tone takes its place. We hear a
new ringing, clear and pure, in the inner ear. The bell may be
silent, but it still rings within us, calling the awareness to prayer.

—⁓—

I am a fountain

stillness—
    in the depths of the lake
    billowing clouds

Issa

English version by David G. Lanoue

stillness ∾

Three lines, just a few syllables each, a moment in time. A great haiku is like peering through a keyhole, the closer we get to it the more we see.

This haiku, for example: We have a still lake reflecting the sky. That's it. That is all the poet gives us. But we understand that it is the lake's stillness that allows it to reflect the sky. The mind, as it constructs this picture for us, expands the relationship between lake and sky to something both universal and personal.

In contemplating the haiku, we watch the scene, and we too receive and reflect an image of beauty. The quieter we become, the clearer the image. We naturally begin to see the lake as our own awareness and the sky as the Eternal. When we are still, the heavens are reflected within our own quiet depths...

—⁓—

look at love
how it tangles
with the one fallen in love

look at spirit
how it fuses with earth
giving it new life
why are you so busy
with this or that or good or bad
pay attention to how things blend

why talk about all
the known and the unknown
see how the unknown merges into the known

why think separately
of this life and the next
when one is born from the last

look at your heart and tongue
one feels but deaf and dumb
the other speaks in words and signs

look at water and fire
earth and wind
enemies and friends all at once

the wolf and the lamb
the lion and the deer
far away yet together

look at the unity of this
spring and winter
manifested in the equinox

you too must mingle my friends
since the earth and the sky
are mingled just for you and me

be like sugarcane
sweet yet silent
don't get mixed up with bitter words

my beloved grows right out of my own heart
how much more union can there be

Rumi

English version by Nader Khalili

Look at love ⁓

> *look at the unity of this*
> *spring and winter*
> *manifested in the equinox*

I first read this poem during the spring equinox. Actually, I had read it before that, but in a cursory way. Then, one day, I read that line about the equinox and it happened to be on the equinox. So I caught myself, paused, and I went back to the beginning to read this poem for the first time.

I began to contemplate the equinox and think about why Rumi mentions it in this poem. The equinox marks the point in the year when the lengths of day and night become equal, when winter gives way to spring or summer to autumn. The equinox is a global transition point. It is a threshold. We release the old and welcome the new as we leave one season behind to begin the new one.

More than at any other time of the year, we are reminded to stand centered on this very moment as we feel how memory reweaves itself into new possibility. It is during the equinox that a new dream is formed—a new vision of ourselves, a new vision of life.

> *why are you so busy*
> *with this or that or good or bad*
> *pay attention to how things blend*

As the equinox joins the past with the future, we have a greater opportunity to see how all things that seem separate, distant, or in conflict, are really a single continuum.

> *the wolf and the lamb*
> *the lion and the deer*
> *far away yet together*

Even life and death, which we imagine to be incompatible opposites, are seen to be different aspects of the same continuity.

> *why think separately*
> *of this life and the next*
> *when one is born from the last*

It is the recognition of this holographic nature in all things that makes the mystic's journey possible, allowing a single experience, a single life to be unpacked in such a way that it reveals to us the entire universe.

the known and the unknown
see how the unknown merges into the known

A journey within the known is no journey at all. But a journey entirely in the unknown leads to disorientation and confusion. A mystic learns to recognize that indistinct threshold, where the known and the unknown merge. We start from there, take our steps with attention, and discover that the borderland between the two moves with us into new territories. We come to recognize that every rise and hollow of the unknown is secretly bordering the known, allowing us to continually reorient and journey on.

This teaches us two things: When we feel lost in life, all we must do is stop, grow still, and see once again familiar territory nearby. The other lesson is that when we feel stuck in what is too familiar, we do not need an elaborate escape to exotic corners of the planet. Wherever we are, we just need to take the unexpected step, and a new path opens before us.

What is most important for us to recognize about any journey is that the destination is contained in the beginning. We don't finally reach our destination; we discover it with each step along the way.

Every journey, if we are paying attention, is an internal journey, a journey within the heart. There opposites meet and melt into each other.

my beloved grows right out of my own heart
how much more union can there be

—∿—

Ha! What is this dance of bliss
Cascading through my senses?
I feel new life, holy rapture
Burning through my nerves and veins.
Was it a god who shaped these symbols
Summoning this inner ecstasy,
Filling my impoverished heart with joy,
And revealing, through some mysterious impulse,
Nature's secret sinews
　　　surrounding me?

Am I a god? I am filled with such light!
In this pure array of emblems I see
Nature's workings laid bare before me.
Only now do I comprehend the sage's wise words:
"The realm of spirit is not barred.
It is your mind that is closed, your heart that is lifeless!
Student, rise without fright,
And bathe your earthly breast
　　　in the rosy dawn's light!"

As all things, one in one, are woven,
Each in the other works and lives and is whole!
While heavenly beings climb and descend
Passing down their golden pails,
And with their incense-pinioned wings
All heaven and earth are blessed;
They sing in symphony
　　　through all things!

Goethe

IMG

105

What is this dance of bliss? ∿

This poem is a selection from Goethe's masterpiece, Faust. The legend of Faust has been in circulation since the early Renaissance and is, in many ways, a foundational myth of modern Western culture. Faust himself is the quintessential mad scientist and modern-day wizard. He is a seeker and a philosopher who oversteps all bounds in his passionate quest. His journey is complex, taking us to uncomfortable places, spiritually and culturally.

Faust's tale, in its bare form, involves a man in search of secret knowledge. The early telling of the Faust legend was framed as a morality tale in which Faust sells his soul to the devil in order to unlock the secrets of nature and gain miraculous powers. This is the classic "Faustian bargain." Amidst the mental and spiritual upheavals of the Renaissance, the story of Faust's magical feats amazed and entertained, while his final downfall reassured audiences with the restoration of social norms.

In the hands of Goethe, however, writing at the beginning of the Age of Enlightenment, Faust's tale is transformed into an exploration of the emerging modern mind at the threshold of unknown realities and uncertain morality.

This new Faust seeks something greater than magical powers, he seeks transcendent knowledge—gnosis. He is desperate to rise above the mundane world, which has been drained of meaning. The old medieval worldview has failed and new truths must be sought by daring minds.

As with Faust's earlier incarnations, Goethe's protagonist still craves secret knowledge, but he is less concerned with gaining magical power over reality as he is with witnessing the hidden truth underlying reality.

Goethe's Faust yearns to behold the whole of existence in one transcendent visionary experience, which he describes as "the sustaining Moment." To attain this, he is willing to sacrifice everything, his old ideas, his place in society, his morality, perhaps even his soul. For this modern Faust, heaven without meaning and transcendence is worse than hell.

Faust is recast as a modern-day Job. Initially, Faust's soul and purpose are pure, so much so that God wagers with the devil that

106

Faust cannot be corrupted. The devil then appears to Faust as Mephistopheles, revealing secret knowledge to Faust, while steadily tempting him away from a strict moral path. That's the tension at the heart of this story, leading to multiple tragedies.

Throughout, we must ask ourselves, is the moral life Faust has abandoned of real value if it was without meaning? Can it even be called a truly moral life, or had he merely been following convention? How far must one step beyond the bounds of social propriety to discover truth? Does the pursuit of truth justify selfishness or harm to others?

Despite his misdeeds and inner turmoil, Goethe's Faust can be seen as heroic. He is at times selfish and cruel, yet he courageously holds to his quest for truth. Faust has been transformed into an anti-hero, championing the newly emerging modern mind that seeks knowledge unshackled by religious and social convention. Faust is desperate to awaken into a new consciousness, to comprehend the hidden workings of reality and his own being, but to do so he must step outside the social order and accepted ways of thinking.

It is telling that, in spite of his deal with the devil and the many tragedies that follow, Goethe's Faust is ultimately welcomed into heaven.

Through Faust, Goethe has given us a manifesto, a proclamation of freedom for the mind and spirit. Yet he does not ignore the darker avenues through which the solitary seeker may stumble on his journey. Goethe is not writing a simple morality tale of good versus evil; instead, he sketches a complex, often cruel world populated by imperfect individuals, and in the midst of that he places a flawed but sincerely seeking individual.

I read Goethe's Faust as a defining meditation on the modern struggle for meaning, genuineness, and identity.

—⁓—

We can read this selection from Goethe's Faust as a template for understanding the ecstatic experience.

> *Ha! What is this dance of bliss*
> *Cascading through my senses?*

The first thing that catches our attention is the way Faust's bliss is not static. It dances, it rushes, it cascades. Bliss is not some flat feeling. It moves and changes. It interacts with us and our own shifting awareness. It is alive.

The description of it flooding through the senses is a reminder that spiritual ecstasy is not some disembodied idea of the mind. Bliss is felt in the body, as well as the soul. Frequently we assume that spiritual experiences are intangible phenomena and, therefore, easily dismissed. But profound experiences of spiritual ecstasy are perceived within every level of one's being, including the physical. It is not inaccurate to say that bliss is sensual as well as spiritual.

Each line here reveals something worth contemplating to better understand spiritual bliss.

> *I feel new life...*

Ecstatic opening, when first experienced, is likened to awakening from a lifelong slumber. It is a complete rebirth and renewal. It is nothing less than new life.

> *Filling my impoverished heart with joy...*

The heart and the breast are referred to several times. In such moments of rapture, the heart is flooded with joy. The heart overflows with an indescribable delight and a radiant love.

> *And revealing, through some mysterious impulse,*
> *Nature's secret sinews*
> *surrounding me*

In his ecstasy, Faust exults more than once at the revelation of nature's secrets. Beyond mere insight into the workings of material nature, he is witness to the nature of reality itself. He glimpses how existence is structured and functions, how it emerges from an underlying foundation of being.

> *Am I a god?*

This is a shocking question to ask in any culture. To some, it seems blasphemous or delusional. Yet mystics keep asking variations of this troubling question.

In states of spiritual ecstasy, the individual sense of self melts into the boundless Divine. Where does one's self end and God begin? Are they separate at all? To proclaim oneself a god in order to feed the ego is obviously narcissistic and delusional, but to honestly give voice to the uncomfortable question at the heart of genuine communion, well, that's uncertain territory. Faust, the iconoclast, brazenly asks the question.

I am filled with such light!

Mystics keep talking of light because light is central to mystical experience. This is the light of being, the light of creation, the light that fills and connects everything, including ourselves. It is the light of enlightenment.

As all things, one in one, are woven,
Each in the other works and lives and is whole!

This is Faust's encapsulation of his vision of unity. He is witness to the workings of nature. He sees that nothing is separate. All things are, in reality, interconnected and have a shared being. In a world that feels broken and in conflict, there is yet an underlying wholeness.

This is the foundational insight of any true mystic. Seeing this, we recognize that, despite surface appearance, all of reality expresses an inherent harmony.

All heaven and earth are blessed;
They sing in symphony
through all things!

For Faust, his moment of ecstasy is not the end of his journey, but his initiation into a deeper phase of seeking and realization. He is then faced with the challenge of how to live according to this new vision, how to embody a stable expression of that reality while still negotiating the complexities and restrictions of society.

Faust takes a road that is at times morally questionable, but his firm commitment to true wisdom ultimately leads him to a heaven that few who follow convention will attain.

In Goethe's Faust the modern seeker has found a flawed but faithful champion.

"...Student, rise without fright,
And bathe your earthly breast
in the rosy dawn's light!"

—⁓—

Tipping Over a Vase

Master Hyakujo decided to found a new monastery, but he had the difficult task of selecting the new abbot from among his disciples.

Calling his disciples together, Hyakujo declared that the person who best answered his question would be named the new abbot. The master filled a vase with water and set it on the ground before the assembled monks. "Who can tell me what this is without naming it?" he challenged.

The senior disciple stepped forward and answered accurately, "No one can call it a wooden shoe."

Then Isan, the lowly cook, shook his head and kicked the vase over, before walking out of the room.

Master Hyakujo laughed and declared, "My senior disciple has been bested." Isan the cook was named the new abbot.

Wu Men

IMG

110

Tipping Over a Vase ～

One way to understand the meaning of this Zen tale is that the water represents Truth or Dharma. The vase is the vessel that holds that truth. It is the teaching. It is the tradition.

That truth, however, cannot be told. Yes, we can use words like "truth" or "reality," or we can fill books with complex philosophical explanations. But ultimately those are all words and do not truly convey what the Truth is. The "water" cannot be named. That is why Master Hyakujo gave this challenge to his disciples.

The lead disciple sees this as a test of his mental dexterity. If he cannot name the water-filled vessel, he will say what it is not, thus suggesting it by negation. But he has only negated one object in a world of countless objects. A person can spend a lifetime listing all the things something is not, and never come to the point where only the unnamed thing remains. The lead disciple is trapped on the endless road of the intellect.

But the cook, Isan, understood the situation plainly. He tipped the vase over, emptying the vessel and revealing the water. The truth cannot be told, it can only be shown.

What's more, the truth cannot be held, it cannot be contained, it can only be poured out. The vase itself, the spiritual tradition, is empty and only has meaning as a vessel to transport the truth. By tipping over the vessel, he is suggesting that we must not worship the tradition itself. Religion, philosophy, spiritual tradition, these are not ends in themselves. They should be respected for their function as a delivery vehicle, but it is what they pour out that gives them value.

These are the insights that mark one for spiritual authority.

—~~—

I am a fountain, You are my water.
I flow from You to You.

I am an eye, You are my light.
I look from You to You.

You are neither my right nor my left.
You are my foot and my arm as well.

I am a traveler, You are my road.
I go from You to You.

Zeynep Hatun

English version by Murat Yagan

I am a fountain, You are my water ∽

I am a fountain, You are my water.

The fountain's structure can represent the individual, the body, the outer form, while the water suggests to us the spirit, the animating life that flows through us, that which gives purpose to the form.

But perhaps this is an overly formal interpretation of the image. The fountain's structure and the water are not truly separate. They work together. The fountain without water is an empty tub with empty pipes. But the water without the fountain is a still pool. We, as individuals, are more than vessels for spirit. We are somehow its living expression. This is a mutual participation, a shared being that brings dancing water to the world.

I flow from You to You.

As we recognize a sense of self at one with the Divine, that self is no longer fixed. Whatever we are, we flow. And wherever we flow, we remain in continuous contact with the Beloved.

I am an eye, You are my light.
I look from You to You.

We imagine that we are individual and separate beings, but it is more accurate to say that we are individual points of perception within one immense, all-encompassing being. The sense of a fixed and separate self can fade, but awareness and the perception of reality remain essential to our nature. We exist in some sense as a divine act of vision, witnesses to creation. And everything we see shines with the light of the Beloved.

You are neither my right nor my left.
You are my foot and my arm as well.

The Divine Beloved is neither here nor there, but everywhere at once, ungraspable. Our very being is of that singular Presence. It fills us, moves us, and gives us life.

I am a traveler, You are my road.
I go from You to You.

On this road, each step, each arc of movement and point of rest, is another instance of contact. We find God all the way to God.

———

Hailstones, too

Worship

Beneath the snows
the hidden world of winter grass.

And in the field of white, a white heron
hides himself.

Dogen

IMG

Worship ~

Looking out my window, I see a quiet winter morning, mist trickling in among the bare branches, yesterday's snow still new upon the ground. I think of this poem...

Reading this poem, we immediately ask what a white heron in snow has to do with worship, as suggested by the title.

> *And in the field of white, a white heron*
> *hides himself.*

Have you ever watched a heron fishing, wading at the edge of a lake? Its entire being is focused. Even when it moves it seems utterly still. Because of these qualities, the heron is a natural symbol for the meditator.

We have a being of white—the heron, the meditator— disappearing into an environment of white—the snow-covered field. In fact, the heron is not passively disappearing, it is actively engaged in the process. He "hides himself" in the snow. How does the heron hide? Through stillness. The heron settles into its own nature. It is already as white as the snowy world it inhabits. The heron just has to grow quiet, be itself, and it naturally disappears from sight.

Snow represents the glowing world as perceived by the enlightened awareness. Everything, when draped in new-fallen snow, becomes one. Everything is the same "white" radiance. Everything comes to rest within this shared glow of being. The idea of separation is lost in that light. Beings and objects are suddenly seen as a fluid continuity within that "field of white."

So this, according to Dogen, is what constitutes true worship: Through meditation and stillness we recognize our own incandescent nature in the midst of the bright field of being. As we settle into ourselves, we gently merge with the luminous reality that surrounds us.

—~—

Held fast in winter's fist,
    water stops flowing.

Running water,
    ice hard as rock,
    or the softness of snow—
three states, but the same substance.

Warmed by the sun of wisdom
they melt down,
    made one once more.

Similarly, self,
    world,
    and all we dream,
melt, traceless,

into the warm embrace of God.

Lalla

IMG

118

Held fast in winter's fist ∽

I spent my later childhood in Los Angeles. I remember a rare day when the temperature dropped to just below freezing. I implored the gods of weather for snow, naïve in my certainty that a single flake of snow was enough to shut down the entire school system. But it was not to be. It was Southern California, after all. No snow, no school closings. Bundled up, I trudged off to school.

So when I moved to Colorado as an adult, you can imagine my sense of wonder at the snow each winter. In fact, I lived in mountain retreats where the snow piled up high enough to block windows and doors, requiring me to dig my way out each morning. Overwhelming but magical!

> *Running water,*
> *   ice hard as rock,*
> *   or the softness of snow—*
> *three states, but the same substance.*

Water becomes solid ice when it is cold enough. It becomes rock-like, impenetrable, tangible. When water is held aloft by clouds and then allowed to fall on a cold day, it reaches earth as snow, in some ways seemingly solid, yet a hand can pass through it. When warmed, ice and snow once again become liquid, flowing and ungraspable. Water in its liquid form loses its sense of being a distinct object. Instead, it takes on the form of the empty space it occupies.

Yet all three—ice, snow, and liquid water—are the same substance. There has been no essential change other than the form perceived by the witness. It only appears to be different.

> *Similarly, self,*
> *   world,*
> *   and all we dream,*
> *melt, traceless,*
>
> *into the warm embrace of God.*

Lalla is reminding us that everything is like this, separate only in apparent form, but in essence one continuity of consciousness. The individual, the world, and God, when seen clearly in the warm light of wisdom "melt down / made one once more."

—⁓—

119

awakened
as ice bursts
the water jar

Basho

English version by Gabriel Rosenstock

awakened ∽

This haiku has sound to it. We can hear the jar crack as it bursts, unable to contain the expanding ice.

The jar holds water in transformation, liquid becoming solid ice.

And—CRACK!—that instant of being startled awake. The haiku stands upon that moment, the liminal space between sleep and wakefulness marked by that sharp sound.

We can, if we choose, catch intimations of enlightenment. Something within has transformed, expanded, burst its container.

We are instantly awake.

—〰—

Hailstones, too,
Enter my begging bowl.

Santoka

English version by John Stevens

Hailstones, too ～

Santoka was a wandering Zen monk at the beginning of the 20th century, and whatever he received in his begging bowl was how he survived the day. For such a monk, the begging bowl is his source of sustenance and also his medium of connection to the wider world. It takes on archetypal significance. The begging bowl becomes the awareness itself. Whatever one receives to nourish body, mind, or soul, comes by way of the begging bowl.

Rice and coin and flowers come to Santoka through his bowl. But it is the monk's discipline to hold out his begging bowl and receive whatever comes to him with equanimity, as the meditator receives with balance whatever passes through his awareness. Hailstones, too, enter the begging bowl. Everything that comes is a gift, food for the spirit, whether or not it satisfies our desires.

To me, this poem evokes that perfect receptivity in which surprise, disillusionment, delight, and new awareness all mix together as the mind opens to what is actually present in the moment.

—✳—

The fire rises in me

As air carries light poured out by the rising sun,
As the candle spills away beneath the flame's touch,
So too does the soul melt when ignited by light,
    its will now gone.
Lost within this light,
    the soul, dying to itself, in majesty lives on.

Why fish among the waves for wine
Spilled into the sea?
It has become the ocean.
Can wine once mingled be drawn again from the water?
So it is with the soul drowned in light:
Love has drunk it in,
changed it, mixed it with truth,
    until it is entirely new.

The soul is willing and yet unwilling,
For there is nothing the soul now seeks,
save for this beauty!
No longer does it hunger or grasp,
    so emptied by such sweetness.
This supreme summit of the soul rises
    from a nothingness shaped
    and set within the Lord.

Jacopone da Todi

IMG

As air carries light ∿

As air carries light poured out by the rising sun,
As the candle spills away beneath the flame's touch,
So too does the soul melt when ignited by light...

With these recognizable images, we begin to get an idea of how
the soul is transformed in exalted states. Flooded by the light of
illumination, we, like wax near a fire, melt. The self is no longer a
fixed, hardened thing, but something fluid and formless. In this
dynamic state, the soul loses its dull opacity, becoming clear,
allowing the light to shine through it.

Lost within this light,
the soul, dying to itself, in majesty lives on.

The old, inanimate self melts away, becoming a new and fluid
being that expresses itself through yielding. In its yielding, the
soul discovers its real life.

So it is with the soul drowned in light:
Love has drunk it in,
changed it, mixed it with truth,
until it is entirely new.

The spiritual concept of surrendering the will is difficult to accept
in any age, but especially so in the modern era when
accomplishment through aggressive exercise of the will is
idolized.

The soul is willing and yet unwilling...

The most immediate objection is that without will, we can do
nothing. On a certain level, we prove our existence by acting in
the world, right?

When deeply examined, however, the will is revealed to be more
complex than we might casually think. There are different
expressions of will. On one level, will is volition or the impulse to
act. Will can be our sense of firm determination. Will is also the
capacity to choose, our free will.

Mystics regularly use terms like "self-will" to express a further
understanding of what the will is and how it works. We can say

126

that self-will is selfish will, as opposed to the willingness to be of service. Or we might say that self-will is willfulness, when we are consumed by our own private purposes and no longer pay attention to feedback from other people or the environment. But there is more to self-will than that.

Self-will isn't always cruel or destructive, at least not in obvious ways. It is quite possible to perform great philanthropic works and still have it be an expression of self-will, for example. Self-will is will that is under the control of the ego. Its actions serve and reinforce the ego. Self-will renews the trance of the ego-self.

Most of what we call will is involved somehow in self-will. But the opposite of self-will is not inaction. There is another form of will that does not originate with the ego and does not constantly return our attention to it. This selfless will is potent, yet it is not our own. To unleash this other will in our lives requires an elegant balance between yielding and stepping forward, between selflessness and presence. We engage in action, but we are not the actors. What we normally think of as the self is not directing the action.

This frees up a great amount of trapped psychic energy, and we become awestruck witnesses to the unexpected grace and power of life acting through us—a vision of immense beauty!

> *For there is nothing the soul now seeks,*
> *save for this beauty!*

—ʌʌ—

The fire rises in me,
    and lights up my heart.
Like the sun!
Like the golden disk!
Opening, expanding, radiant—
    Yes!
      —a flame!

I say again:
    I don't know
    what to say!

I'd fall silent
—If only I could—
but this marvel
    makes my heart leap,
it leaves me open-mouthed
    like a fool,

urging me
    to summon words
    from my silence.

Symeon the New Theologian

IMG

128

The fire rises in me 〜

This is a poem of fire and silence. Why fire? In spiritual ecstasy there is often a rising sense of heat—filled with boundless love— that permeates the body. This spiritual fire seems to emerge from the seat, warming the belly and expanding the heart as it climbs upward.

> *The fire rises in me,*
> *and lights up my heart.*

As this fire moves through the body, it also moves through the awareness, consuming all thoughts.

With thoughts stilled, the mind at rest, what is left to say?

> *I say again:*
> *I don't know*
> *what to say!*

This fire burns away even the thought of "I." Even the limited idea of self is found to be merely one more thought that can fall silent. Only the living flame remains.

Everything has been turned inside out. We ourselves have been remade, revealing every detail in beauty. What can we do but gape in awe?

> *it leaves me open-mouthed*
> *like a fool...*

The heart, giddy within this widening vista of bliss, naturally yearns to share its joy at witnessing "this marvel." Though the world has become wordless, words somehow rise from the deep silence—

> *urging me*
> *to summon words*
> *from my silence.*

—〜〜—

The Soul that rises with us, our life's Star,
     Hath had elsewhere its setting,
          And cometh from afar:
     Not in entire forgetfulness,
     And not in utter nakedness,
But trailing clouds of glory do we come
     From God, who is our home.

William Wordsworth

The Soul that rises with us ∿

This selection from Wordsworth's "Intimations of Immortality" is one of those rare poetic utterances that brings us to a full stop with its sumptuous beauty.

Some poems sacrifice substance in their confection of words and imagery. That can be its own delight. But this poem combines an expanding awareness with its luxuriant language, and it all comes together in a way that invites a sigh of appreciation.

At times I read these words and think the language is almost overripe. But no, not quite. It holds. And then I am carried away again.

Its first few lines distill the soul's feelings of loneliness and vulnerability, the sense that something important in one's very being has been hidden from memory. But in giving voice to this anxiety, the poem gently negates it, emphasizing the word "not"—

> *Not in entire forgetfulness,*
> *And not in utter nakedness*

We are not entirely lost.

The poem resuscitates our imperfect memory of self with those final lush lines—

> *But trailing clouds of glory do we come*
> *From God, who is our home.*

We are recollected, restored, as clouds of glory trail from our shoulders. We come home.

—∿—

Marriage of the Soul

The Marriage of the Soul

Descending to the earth, that strange intoxicating beauty of the
    unseen world
lurks in the elements of nature.

And the soul of man,
who has attained the rightful balance,
becoming aware of this hidden joy,
straightaway is enamored and bewitched.

And from this mystic marriage are born
the poets' songs, inner knowledge,
the language of the heart, virtuous living,
and the fair child Beauty.

And the Great Soul gives to man as dowry
the hidden glory of the world.

Shabistari

English version by Florence Lederer

The Marriage of the Soul ∼

> *Descending to the earth, that strange intoxicating beauty of the unseen
> world
> lurks in the elements of nature.*

Shabistari draws us in with his description of the "intoxicating
beauty" of the divine presence hidden within the physical world of
nature.

> *And the soul of man,
> who has attained the rightful balance,
> becoming aware of this hidden joy,
> straightaway is enamored and bewitched.*

As we, through spiritual practice, attain "the rightful balance,"
we begin to perceive that presence within everything,
everywhere, most importantly within ourselves. And, perhaps
surprisingly, we discover that it is filled with a "hidden joy." This
recognition of the divine presence everywhere is accompanied by
a flood of bliss and pure delight. How then can a lover of God not
be "enamored and bewitched"?

> *And from this mystic marriage are born
> the poets' songs, inner knowledge,
> the language of the heart, virtuous living,
> and the fair child Beauty.*

This is the moment that various traditions refer to as the mystic
marriage, the *unio mystica*—Union. This moment of profoundest
oneness between the individual soul and the universal spirit is
the root experience of all spirituality. It is commonly pointed out
that the word "yoga" means to yoke or to join... in union, but we
forget that the word "religion" also means to reconnect or rejoin.
They are essentially the same word. Every religion and spiritual
tradition is built upon union.

That mystic marriage is not just a superficial feeling of
connectedness and joy. Something is unlocked within the
individual. The mystic perceives himself or herself differently.
Reality itself is reformed in the awareness. At the same time,
unexpected gifts and creativity are unlocked within the renewed
soul. Not uncommonly, mystics begin to write poetry... or, if they
have been writing all along, their verses take on a new life and a

deeper resonance that carries the breath of the mysteries. (This is why there is an overlap in the ancient world between poetry and mysticism.)

Mystics also speak of "knowledge" or gnosis, but this is not knowledge in the sense of information. While it is true that one's intuition may be heightened, the knowledge referred to here is more of a fullness of awareness. It is as if one floats in the ocean of knowingness. An all-encompassing meaning and interrelationship becomes the fluid substance of being, a living consciousness that fills and unifies all of existence within its own immense self-awareness.

The disparate parts within the individual are unified as well. It is an interior marriage as much as an exterior marriage. This spiritual union leads to the recognition of a grand harmony equally within oneself and throughout creation.

> *And the Great Soul gives to man as dowry*
> *the hidden glory of the world.*

The pervading beauty and harmony, the creativity and knowledge, the centering within the full self, all of this is the wedding gift, which, in turn, becomes the mystic's gift to the world.

—∾∾—

Preparing to Greet the Goddess

Do not think of her
unless you are prepared
to be driven to your limits,
to rush forth from yourself
like a ritual bowl overflowing
with sacramental wine.

Do not summon her image
unless you are ready to be blinded,
to stand in the flash
of a center exploding,
yourself shattering into the landscape,
wavering bits of bark and water.

Do not speak her name
until you have said good-bye
to all your familiar trinkets—
your mirrors, your bracelets,
your childhood adorations—
From now on you are nothing,
a ghost sighing at the window,
a voice singing under water.

Dorothy Walters

Preparing to Greet the Goddess ∾

Do not think of her
unless you are prepared
to be driven to your limits...

We like our goddesses gentle. We prefer them maternal and comforting. We want them tame. But the Divine Feminine can also be shattering in her love. She can be ferocious in her destruction of our cherished illusions. The realization she bestows can be blissful or devastating—or both simultaneously.

Dorothy Walters has written extensively about her unexpected Kundalini awakening, a profoundly transformative experience that imbues much of her poetry. The mysterious Goddess we are preparing to greet is Kundalini herself.

According to yogic descriptions of the energetic body, we all carry within us a powerful spiritual energy, typically dormant at the base of the spine. This is the Kundalini Shakti. It is considered to be a manifestation of the sacred feminine principle within each individual. For this reason, the Kundalini is referred to as a goddess. Through spiritual practice, profound inner stillness, or occasionally through trauma, the fiery Kundalini can be roused from her slumber to rise up the spine, where she merges with the masculine energy seated in the crown. This blissful union between the two energetic poles opens the individual psyche beyond the limits of the ego. This experience clears the pathway to enlightenment and spiritual liberation.

Do not summon her image
unless you are ready...

But this energetic opening should not be invited casually. The ideal is to, first, patiently cultivate inner balance and self-awareness. This is because the transformative fire of the Kundalini is fierce. Its action reveals the hidden fissures within the ego's façade. Even when preceded by sincere spiritual work, the Kundalini's awakening shakes apart our cherished ideas about who we are.

This is why the poet admonishes us to not even think of the Goddess until we are prepared to be driven to our limits, that is, until we are ready to go beyond our restricted ideas of who we are.

The Goddess Kundalini, through her blazing heat, sends the idea of the ego-self "shattering into the landscape." Yet, even within that fiery blast, we remain. Who we really are, our essential Self, is finally revealed, standing in the center of that blinding flash of light.

Dorothy Walters is, I think, urging us to prepare earnestly, reverently for the rising Kundalini, rather than frivolously seeking the thrill of a new experience. When we "greet the Goddess," we can no longer cling to the "familiar trinkets" with which we surround ourselves to bolster the ego's tenuous existence. The poet gives us that evocative closing image in which the limited self is finally seen as "nothing / a ghost sighing at the window." It is a mere suggestion of existence that is already fading as we watch it.

Encountering the Goddess, the old self we thought we were vanishes. We discover that we are something utterly new, a being filled to overflowing with the sweetness of the universe—

> *like a ritual bowl overflowing*
> *with sacramental wine.*

—◈—

The Union of Shiva and Shakti

I offer obeisance to the God and Goddess,
The limitless primal parents of the universe.

They are not entirely the same,
Nor are they not the same.
We cannot say exactly what they are.

How sweet is their union!
The whole world is too small to contain them,
Yet they live happily in the smallest particle.

These two are the only ones
Who dwell in this home called the universe.
When the Master of the house sleeps,
The Mistress stays awake
And performs the functions of both.

When He awakes, the whole house disappears,
And nothing at all is left.

Two lutes: one note.
Two flowers: one fragrance.
Two lamps: one light.

Two lips: one word.
Two eyes: one sight.
These two: one universe.

In unity there is little to behold;
So She, the mother of abundance,
Brought forth the world as play.

He takes the role of Witness
Out of love of watching Her.
But when Her appearance is withdrawn,
The role of Witness is abandoned as well.

Through Her,
He assumes the form of the universe;

139

Without Her,
He is left naked.

If night and day were to approach the Sun,
Both would disappear.
In the same way, their duality would vanish
If their essential Unity were seen.

In fact, the duality of Shiva and Shakti
Cannot exist in that primal unitive state
From which AUM emanates.

They are like a stream of knowledge
From which a knower cannot drink
Unless he gives up himself.

Is the sound of AUM divided into three
Simply because it contains three letters?
Or is the letter 'N' divided into three
because of the three lines by which it is formed?

So long as Unity is undisturbed,
And a graceful pleasure is thereby derived,
Why should not the water find delight
In the floral fragrance of its own rippled surface?

It is in this manner I bow
To the inseparable Shiva and Shakti.

A man returns to himself
When he awakens from sleep;
Likewise, I have perceived the God and Goddess
By waking from my ego.

When salt dissolves,
It becomes one with the ocean;
When my ego dissolved,
I became one with Shiva and Shakti.

Jnaneshwar

English version by Swami Abhayananda

140

The Union of Shiva and Shakti ～

I offer obeisance to the God and Goddess,
The limitless primal parents of the universe.

In Hindu metaphysics, the primal duality is expressed in terms of
the pairing of god and goddess, the masculine and feminine forms
of the Eternal. That union and tension between the divine male
and female permeates and defines all levels of reality. Shiva, the
male in this pairing, represents the transcendent essence. The
feminine Shakti is the universal essence expressing itself through
sound and vibration in order to manifest existence.

This is the dance of duality and nonduality that occurs
throughout the universe, among galaxies, within individuals,
even within the particles of the atom.

On the human level, Shiva is experienced as resting in the energy
center of the crown, while Shakti is the Kundalini force that
typically lies dormant at the base of the spine. When the latent
Kundalini Shakti is awakened, this powerful energy rises to the
crown and joins in union with Shiva. This union of divine male
and female energies within the individual is the "spiritual
marriage" that initiates enlightenment and bliss—

How sweet is their union!

Everything embodies this eternal dynamic. Everything has its
essence along with the expression of that essence. And the
expression is always seeking to reunite with its essence. Matter is
always seeking union with Spirit. But on careful examination, we
recognize that the two, in fact, have never been separate. There is
no dividing line. They exist together, essence and expression, like
a fire and the heat it radiates.

When we understand this metaphysical language, the poem opens
up into a precise description of the subtle nature of reality. "They
are not entirely the same," because distinctions can be made
between these two aspects of the Divine. "Nor are they not the
same," because their duality is a purely conceptual distinction.
(Does fire exist without heat? Does heat exist without its source?
Can we truly speak of fire apart from heat? We should more
accurately speak of fire-heat as a single thing. The distinction is
an artificial separation.) "We cannot say exactly what they are,"

because the truth is beyond the ability of the intellect to formulate into words. Truth cannot be fully encapsulated in words, it can only be perceived directly.

> *When He awakes, the whole house disappears,*
> *And nothing at all is left.*

When we come to recognize this essential nature of reality, all things are seen to be interconnected expressions emerging from the same universal essence. Amidst this vision of unity, the distinction between things blurs. Form and space may still be perceived, but they are seen as empty, illusory. We no longer see in separated objects. The "thingness" of things is lost. "Nothing at all is left." One sees the idea of objects, but there are no actual objects to see.

> *In unity there is little to behold...*

This perception of reality as being empty of anything external or isolated is said to be the reason for duality in the first place. The undivided Eternal assumes the pretense of duality in order to create a vantage point from which to see the rich diversity and movement of manifesting reality:

> *He takes the role of Witness*
> *Out of love of watching Her.*

It is a form of love play, a game of hide-and-seek the Divine plays with itself. The One pretends to be two, perceiver and perceived, allowing observation and celebration of its own nature.

Within this play of awareness we have our entire existence. We humans, and all things, are born of awareness. Our very nature is that playful awareness.

But, ultimately, the game of duality, of actor and witness, collapses in on itself, and the truth of unity can be denied no longer. Shiva and Shakti are, in reality, "inseparable." They are not two, but One. The crown and the Kundalini's seat are not separated by some distance of space along the spine; they are two poles within the same being—you! (How can the fire be separate from its heat?)

142

When we finally tire of the game of duality, then we are able to settle into the recognition that there is only unity and nothing else.

> *It is in this manner I bow*
> *To the inseparable Shiva and Shakti.*

Composed of Nows

If you keep seeking the jewel of understanding,
then you are a mine of understanding in the making.
If you live to reach the Essence one day,
then your life itself is an expression of the Essence.
Know that in the final analysis you are that
which you search for.

Abu-Said Abil-Kheir

English version by Vraje Abramian

If you keep seeking the jewel of understanding ∿

This poem speaks a truth that should be obvious, but somehow isn't.

> *If you live to reach the Essence one day,*
> *then your life itself is an expression of the Essence.*

When we focus on a goal, when we turn all our thoughts and energies toward it, we take on the qualities of that for which we strive. We could say that we become what we seek, but that is not exactly what Abu-Said Abil-Kheir is saying. We don't become what we seek; we discover that we already are that. What we seek we find within. It has always been there. We simply must search.

When we are reminded of this truth, a hidden tension in the soul eases. There is always that nagging question at the beginning of our journey: Will I achieve my goal? Am I foolish to even pursue it? This poem's insight dismantles that self-defeating inner dialogue. Through seeking we necessarily succeed. The seeking itself defines us and opens us, awakening recognition of the goal within.

> *Know that in the final analysis you are that*
> *which you search for.*

—∿—

Sometimes
    I go about pitying myself.

Yet all the while
    I am carried by winds
    across the sky.

Ojibway Song

IMG

Sometimes ∿

Usually, all it takes is a shift in perspective.

We frequently feel hurt or angry or sad or just trapped. The common response, especially in our task-oriented modern era, is to decide what we are going to do about it. We try to take charge. We act, we do, we fix. And, yes, that approach can be useful in many circumstances.

But we need to make sure we don't 'do' as a way to avoid feeling. Frequently we have an impulse toward action because, otherwise, we will have to feel, and what we actually feel may not be pleasant or contained. But if we don't feel fully, some part of ourselves has been shut down, separated from the whole, and our field of perception has narrowed.

That's the other reason not to rush to action. 'Doing' can become a way to reinforce our limited ideas about reality. Action is like a ritual, it makes everything feel more real, more imprinted in the mind. This can be a good thing or it can be a trap. It depends on whether or not we are seeing clearly.

In any situation, the first thing to do is to not do anything. Instead, we should first allow our perspective to shift. We must see what we see. This is the most potent act possible. Seemingly doing nothing, all of reality changes. The willingness to step aside from our own internal dramas allows us to recognize and utilize the great currents already flowing soundlessly through our lives. Then, in harmony with that underlying momentum, should we choose to act, our actions have a power and purpose, bringing extraordinary results.

We soar, we dance, we are carried by winds across the sky.

—∿—

The Tenth Man

A wise guru lived with ten disciples, all young men from the same village across the river. A festival time drew near and the disciples sought their guru's permission to cross the river and celebrate with their families.

The guru decided to test his disciples. He claimed that he was unable to accompany them because he had to leave immediately on an important errand but, after a show of reluctance, he gave his consent for them to travel to their home village.

As the ten young men crossed the river in their small boat, a terrible storm rose up. The boat was overturned and they were tossed into the river. As they separately scrambled to shore, wet and coughing, they regrouped to make sure everyone was safe.

The eldest of the group assumed the role of leader and lined everyone up in order to count them: "One, two, three, four, five, six, seven, eight... nine." He only counted nine, forgetting to count himself.

The young men were frantic. They reorganized their line and their leader counted again, but again he counted only nine. They tried several times, and each time only counted nine.

The disciples began to cry out for help as they ran along the shore hoping to save their lost friend.

Unbeknownst to the young men, their guru had secretly crossed the river ahead of them and had witnessed the entire scene from his hiding place. When he emerged and approached his distraught students, they threw themselves at their guru's feet crying over their drowned brother.

To their shock, their guru laughed and informed them that the tenth man was alive. Further, he told them that, through his great *siddhi* powers, he would return the missing disciple. In fact, the lost youth would magically appear in their very midst.

Desperate, they asked for their guru's help to save their friend.

The guru had them line up once again, with the eldest of the young men at the end. Their teacher went down the line and, as he counted aloud, he gave each a slap on the chest to remove all doubt that each had been counted once and only once. "One, two, three, four, five, six, seven, eight, nine…" and coming at last to the group's leader, the guru exclaimed with a final whack, "Ten!"

Astonished and relieved, the disciples shouted with joy. "We are reunited!" they exclaimed. "Our guru truly is a great *siddha*!"

Between bouts of laughter, their guru explained what had happened, that the tenth man had never drowned and had always been with them. Their young leader had forgotten to count himself.

Traditional Hindu Adviata Story

IMG

The Tenth Man   〜

One of the best-known versions of this story was told by the 20th century Indian nondualist sage, Ramana Maharshi.

The Hindu tradition of nondualism, known as Advaita Vedanta, recognizes the transcendent reality to be one's very self. This is not the surface or ego self we normally imagine ourselves to be, but the fully realized Self of selves. The question this insight raises is, if the Divine is somehow our own being, why don't we automatically recognize that divinity within ourselves all the time? Why do we search and strain and still feel bereft?

From the point-of-view of Ramana Maharshi's nondualism, the problem is not a lack of dedication or holiness. Neither is it a problem of finding the right sect or practice or teacher. The real issue is a problem of perspective: The eye is capable of seeing everything except itself, as illustrated by this story.

The story of "The Tenth Man" invites us to laugh at the misperception common to our spiritual efforts. The young disciples might be understood to represent aspects of the seeker's awareness. Their leader—the tenth man—is the *ahamkara*, frequently translated as the "I-maker." This is the ego, the aspect of the mind that inserts itself into the center of every drama, attempting to take charge. This stumbling leader, when forgetful and outward focused, is full of bluster and fear, and no matter how hard he tries, he is unable to find what is missing. The matter can only be resolved when enlightened awareness, represented by the guru, sees the full picture and emerges from hiding to restore perspective.

We are so used to the vague but constant sense of "me," that it fades into the background of awareness. Our own being is so obvious to us that we become blind to it. We know it is there, it must be, but because of its ubiquitous presence, we rarely come to know the self at all. Instead, we filter out our real self from our surface awareness in order to better engage with the demanding, rapidly shifting details that make up our daily lives. Still there is that ache, that sense of missing something essential.

Determined to be whole again, we look everywhere, growing more desperate, but we can't find that lost something. If we are lucky, someone reminds us to look within. If we are really lucky, we

151

understand and once again recognize the self that has been with us all along. In reality, it is not "with" us at all; rather, it *is* us. It is who and what we are in our wholeness. What is most surprising is that this overlooked full sense of who we are is much more than we ever imagined. It is immense and filled with bliss and somehow fundamentally interwoven with the Eternal.

This is when the ten men are "reunited," though, of course, the joke is that no one was ever lost. All of that fear and heartache had nothing to do with the reality of the situation. What seemed like a tragedy is revealed to have been a comedy. All that was needed was a change in perspective that allowed the situation to be seen clearly, enabling the ten men to finally recognize the wholeness they always were.

—~~~—

Forever—is composed of Nows—
'Tis not a different time—
Except for Infiniteness—
And Latitude of Home—

From this—experienced Here—
Remove the Dates—to These—
Let Months dissolve in further Months—
And Years—exhale in Years—

Without Debate—or Pause—
Or Celebrated Days—
No different Our Years would be
From Anno Domini's—

Emily Dickinson

Forever—is composed of Nows ∾

Although Emily Dickinson is rightly praised as one of the great American poets, less commonly is she recognized as a mystic describing states of ecstatic awareness. If her poetry had been composed in India, she would have a place alongside the other great poet-saints, like Lalla and Mirabai.

Forever—is composed of Nows—

Forever, eternity, and, by extension, heaven... Whether we think of eternity as a place or time or even a state of awareness, we set it beyond our reach. We imagine that eternity must be attained, that it is something not here, but elsewhere, in the future. Thinking this way, forever is never found.

Emily Dickinson reveals an essential insight: Forever—is composed of Nows. The future is only an idea. When we reach it, has become the present. Time is not composed of past, present, and future. It is composed of now, and now, and now. We have memories of the past and imaginings about the future, but we only ever experience now.

When we thoroughly understand this, we cease turning back to a remembered past or reaching out for a desired future. We finally come to rest in the present moment. And we are shocked to discover how little we have known of this world of Now, though it is our only home.

All the months and years of the past, the numberless days stretching into the future, all the experiences they hold, pour into the present and fill it. The present expands to hold all of reality along with our undivided selves. Each year, each moment of each year, is a vast blissful space awaiting discovery.

We don't need to look to the future or the past for Anno Domini, the Year of the Lord, we need to look profoundly into Now.

I will add that this is a particular problem with the framing of religious events using historical language—from the coming of the Messiah or the Mahdi or Maitreya to the Resurrection or some future golden age. Regardless of what the calendar says, these events don't exist in the past or the future, they always exist right now.

154

When we look for our spiritual utopia in past history or future possibilities, we ignore the present and fail to find it. The more desperate we become to experience the promised paradise, the more we adopt an ends-justify-the-means mentality to force its historical advent. The terrible irony is that this approach tends to create a hellish present that prevents us from experiencing the heaven we seek.

When we are truly ready to discover our Forever, we will stop our cruelties and give up the agony that drives them. We will sit, become quiet, and finally know Anno Domini—right now.

> *No different Our Years would be*
> *From Anno Domini's—*

—〰—

Right here it is eternally full and serene,
If you search elsewhere, you cannot see it.
You cannot grasp it, you cannot reject it;
In the midst of not gaining,
In that condition you gain it.

Yoka Genkaku

English version by Robert Aitken

Right here it is eternally full and serene ～

Right here it is eternally full and serene,
If you search elsewhere, you cannot see it.

What is it we are seeking? Enlightenment? Salvation? Heaven?
God? If something is missing, then it must be somewhere else. So
we seek out new groups, new teachers, new religions, new lands.
Even in our meditation and prayer, we are reaching, reaching
out—for what?

It seems insulting to our efforts to be told that what we have
sought for so long is "right here." If it was already here, we would
feel it and know it, right?

Yet, insulting or not, it is absolutely true: What we seek is right
here. Not elsewhere. Not in the future. Right here.

Which begs the question, if this all-important enlightening
something is always at hand, why does it elude us? First, because
it is so difficult for the mind to accept that this thing we seek is
not a thing at all. It cannot be grasped or held or claimed. It is not
an object outside of ourselves. It is not a thing contained within
space or time or even within ideas. It is not a thing that starts
and ends, nor is it here but not there; rather, it is an effulgence of
awareness. Even that might suggest to us that it is something
within the mind to be coaxed forth, which implies a phenomenon
that has a beginning and, therefore, an end.

It would be easy to dismiss all of this as philosophical wordplay
were it not for the fact that we are told repeatedly that solving
this riddle unlocks a whole new self and a whole new reality. If we
accept even the possibility that enlightenment/heaven/God are
not only knowable, but the actual state of reality, then to dismiss
such wordplay is foolish in the extreme.

Since sage voices keep telling us that what we seek is right here
and not elsewhere, I suggest we try an experiment: Let us stop
imagining another place or another experience. Let us stop trying
to imagine what it is we seek at all. If we ache, let us feel it
intensely without imagining what will soothe it. Let us, instead,
grow quiet and drop all the mind's imaginings. And then let us
see. What do we notice? Not trying to grasp or gain or escape,

what do we sense right here? What has been consistently present that we have always felt but never noticed?

> *In the midst of not gaining,*
> *In that condition you gain it.*

The mysterious touch we feel might just surprise us—right here.

—◦∿◦—

Through and Through

You are my true self, O Lord.
>My pure awareness is your consort.
>My breath, my body are your handmaids.
I am your holy ground.

My every action is an offering to you.
>My rest is my merging with you.
Every step I take circles you.
>Every word I speak is a song for you.

Whatever work I do,
>that work is worship of you,
>>O Fountain of Bliss!

Shankara

IMG

—m—

Steadfast friend,
You have hewn me
>through and through!

When I speak, my every word
>speaks of you.
And when silent,
>silently I ache for you.

Rabia

IMG

160

Gray, my friend, is every theory,
but green is the glowing tree of life.

Goethe

IMG

Afterword

A poem does not wish to be analyzed. It invites us to engage with it, to interact with it, and to allow ourselves to be transformed by that process.

The magic of a poem is not found in its words or its structure, but in our response to it. A good poem is not external, it exists inside of us.

I share the commentaries accompanying these poems in that same spirit. I do not intend them to be absolute explanations. Poems change with us. Their meanings evolve as our own perspective and understandings change. Can any single explanation encompass such a living, responsive thing? The thoughts and commentaries I include with each poem are offered as a way to encourage your own conversations with the poets gathered here.

I hope you will make a place for these poems in your daydreams and meditations. Watch how you change in the presence of these mysterious, ecstatic songs of realization—and see how they change with you, revealing new insights and hidden moments of bliss.

—*∿*—

About the Poets

Abu-Said Abil-Kheir (Turkmenistan, 967 – 1049)
Shaikh Abu-Said Abil-Kheir was a Sufi who famously referred to himself as "Nobody, Son of Nobody" to convey the mystic's sense of having merged with the Divine, leaving no trace of the ego behind. He lived in what is modern day Turkmenistan, just north of Iran and Afghanistan in Central Asia.

Ansari (Afghanistan, 1006 – 1088)
Shaikh Khwaja Abdullah Ansari was born in Herat, in western Afghanistan. Although his father was a shopkeeper, Ansari was well educated in traditional subjects, such as law and *hadith*, as well as a revered authority on Islamic mysticism and philosophy. He shunned the company of the wealthy and powerful in favor of sharing his wisdom among the common people. His writings and collected sayings continue to inspire Sufis and seekers today.

Arapaho (US)
The Arapaho are a plains nation whose traditional homelands are in Colorado and Wyoming. There is some uncertainty in attributing this Ghost Dance Song selection to the Arapaho people. The originally published source is unclear in its attribution, leaving open the possibility that part or all of this selection comes from the Lakota Sioux.

Basho (Japan, 1644 – 1694)
Matsuo Basho took his name from the Japanese word for "banana tree." He was given a banana tree as a gift by a student, and the poet immediately identified with the small tree and its large, awkward leaves. Basho was born in 1644 near Kyoto, Japan. His father was a poor samurai-farmer. As a teenager, he entered the service of the local lord, acting as his page. The young lord was only a couple of years older than Basho, and the two became friends, enjoying the exchange of haiku verses. While both were still young, his friend died. Basho was devastated and left home, abandoning his samurai status and taking to a life of travel. Some years later, he settled in Edo (Tokyo), where he wrote and published his poetry. His haiku began to attract attention and students gathered around him. At about this time, he also took up Zen meditation. Basho remained restless, even in his fame. A neighborhood fire left him homeless, and he once again took up the itinerant life, visiting friends and students. During this time Basho composed some of his greatest haiku. Basho died in Edo in 1694, having returned just a few years earlier.

Constantine P. Cavafy (Egypt, 1863 – 1933)
Constantine P. Cavafy was born in Alexandria, Egypt to parents who were culturally Greek and originally from Constantinople (Istanbul). Constantine was still a boy when his father died, leaving the family's business of international trade in a precarious position. The family relocated to England to shore up the business, now run by Constantine's oldest brother, but it eventually failed, causing financial hardships and further family moves during Constantine's youth. Cavafy eventually returned to Alexandria in his 20s, finding work in the government's public works department, a position he held for thirty years. During this period, he wrote poetry and sent it to friends and fellow writers. Although he

came to be recognized as a great poet among Greek communities, it was only in the few years before his death that he began to gain notoriety in the rest of the world, particularly for his best-known poem, "Ithaca." Cavafy died from throat cancer in 1933. It is said that his last action was to draw a circle with a dot at its center on a piece of paper.

Chiyo-ni (Japan, 1703 – 1775)
Fukuda Chiyo-ni showed a childhood gift for poetry and gained fame for her haiku while she was still a teenager. Her early haiku were influenced by Basho and his students, though, as her skill grew, she developed her own unique style. Chiyo-ni became a nun of the Pure Land Buddhist sect.

Andrew Colliver (Australia, 1953 –)
Andrew Colliver is a psychiatric social worker living in rural New South Wales in Australia. He writes, "In 2006, the experience—now happening to thousands across the globe—of consciousness awakening to itself within the human form, began to upend my life, and also to seek expression in words. Ideas and words come most frequently when I'm in nature, but any setting can be seen at any time for what it is: the expression of undivided consciousness."

Emily Dickinson (United States, 1830 – 1886)
Emily Dickinson was born to a prominent family in Amherst, Massachusetts. Despite literary anonymity during her lifetime, Dickinson has come to be regarded as one of the greatest of American poets. Her unusual use of rhyme, meter, and grammar anticipates trends in modern poetry. Dickinson was a critic of the common practice of religion in her day, yet she experienced a rich inner life that she understood in religious terms. Much of her poetry meditates on heaven and the inner life, contrasting the private moment against religious convention. If one reads her poetry side-by-side with the poet-saints of India and elsewhere, the parallels in metaphoric language and insight are striking. Much is made of Dickinson's reclusive life, the fact that she never married, and the focus on death in her poetry, leading to characterizations of her as a morbid, sexually repressed recluse. Recognizing the depth of her inner life, however, we can view her as an urban mystic and contemplative poet of the highest order.

Dionysius the Areopagite (Syria, 6th century)
The writings of Dionysius the Areopagite, (also called Denys or Pseudo-Dionysius) have had a profound impact on mystical Christianity, both in the West and in Eastern Orthodox traditions. It is not an exaggeration to say that nearly all Christian mystical movements from the medieval era through the Renaissance and even into modern times have been directly or indirectly influenced by his writings. He is referred to as Pseudo-Dionysius by scholars because the name Dionysius is a reference to one of Paul's Athenian converts mentioned in the Book of Acts. Dionysius the Areopagite clearly lived several centuries after the Dionysius of Acts, borrowing the name as a spiritual mantle. Little is known for certain about who this second Dionysius was, though scholars speculate that he was a Syrian monk who lived around the 6th century.

Dogen (Japan, 1200 – 1253)
Eihei Dogen, respectfully referred to as Dogen Zenji, was a key figure in the development of Japanese Zen practice. Dogen was born about 1200 in Kyoto, Japan. At the age of 17, he was formally ordained as a Buddhist monk.

Considering the Japanese Buddhism of the time to be corrupt and influenced by secular power struggles, Dogen traveled to China to discover the heart of the tradition by studying Ch'an (Zen) Buddhism at several ancient monasteries. Dogen returned to Japan in 1236. He left the politicized environment of Kyoto, however, and settled in the mountains of remote Echizen Province, where he established his own school of Zen, the Soto school. While he was a talented writer and poet, the core of Dogen's teaching was to transcend the mind's addiction to language and form in order to become fully present and recognize one's inherent enlightenment.

Johann Wolfgang von Goethe (Germany, 1749 – 1832)
Johann Wolfgang von Goethe was a poet, playwright, novelist, scientist, statesman, and artist whose cultural significance can be compared with Shakespeare, Cervantes, or Dante. He was born to an upper middle-class family in Frankfurt. As a student, Goethe experienced a life-threatening illness, possibly tuberculosis. Shaken by this brush with death, he began to explore a range of ideas and philosophies from evangelical Christianity to alchemy. While still in his 20s, Goethe attained literary fame for an early novel. He became associated with the *Sturm und Drang* movement, which laid the foundations for European Romanticism. At the invitation of Duke Karl August, Goethe settled in Weimar, where he acted as the Duke's friend and political advisor. Goethe did not marry until his 50s, when he wed his longtime mistress, with whom he had already had several children. Because of his literary prominence alongside his political connections, Goethe was witness to and, in some cases, a participant in the major political and social upheavals in Europe of the early modern era. He lived long enough to become a revered cultural icon during his lifetime, and he has profoundly influenced subsequent generations of writers, artists, philosophers, and seekers.

Ayn al-Quzat Hamadani (Persia/Iran, 1098 – 1131)
Ayn al-Quzat Hamadani (sometimes transliterated as Ayn al-Qozat or Ayn-al-Qudat Hamadani) was a Sufi philosopher, mystic, mathematician, and a judge. He was born in northern Persia (Iran). The name Hamadani is a reference to his family roots in the city of Hamadan. One popular tradition says that, as a boy Hamadani studied with Omar Khayyam when the great mathematician and poet traveled through the region. Hamadani became a young leader of Sufi philosophical thought, advancing a more systematic view of Sufism. Hamadani was executed in Baghdad at the age of 33 on the charge of heresy. Hamadani, Hallaj, and Suhrawardi are often linked as Sufi masters who were martyred for expressing truths authorities found too uncomfortable to hear.

Zeynep Hatun (Turkey, 15th century)
Zeynep Hatun was one of the first significant women voices of Ottoman poetry. She wrote a *diwan* (a collection of poetry), which has been lost. The limited sources of information we have about her disagree on her place of birth, but there is agreement that she lived some portion of her life in Istanbul. Camille Helminski writes in *Women of Sufism*: *"Zeynep Hatun [was] one of the strong women of Sufism around whom people have gathered for light and guidance in the Ankara region of Turkey for many years..."*

166

Hildegard von Bingen (Germany, 1098 – 1179)

At the age of eight, Hildegard was "given to God as a tithe" when she was placed in the care of a local holy woman. Hildegard took monastic vows in her teens and eventually became the head of her monastic community. She had a natural gift of clairvoyance and was a respected healer and herbalist, having written works on natural history and the medicinal uses of plants. Her two great spiritual works are *Scivias*, a collection of revelatory visions on humanity, nature, and God, and the *Symphonia*, which gathers together her music and poetry. Her fame was widespread during her lifetime, and she went on several teaching tours through the Rhineland.

Friedrich Holderlin (Germany, 1770 – 1843)

Friedrich Holderlin was born in the region of Swabia in southwestern Germany. As a young man, Holderlin attended the Theological Seminary in Tubingen, where he became friends with the philosopher Hegel and the poet/dramatist Friedrich von Schiller. During the 1790s he went through a period of inspired creativity, crafting many great poems and his novel *Hyperion*. In the early 1800s, he suffered a nervous collapse, triggered in part by the death of a married woman with whom he had fallen in love. He returned to his childhood home of Swabia to recuperate. During his recovery, he came to live with the family of a local carpenter—and he chose to live with them for the rest of his life, more than 35 additional years.

Marie Howe (United States, 1950 –)

Marie Howe received her MFA from Columbia University, studying with Stanley Kunitz. In the late 1980s, her brother died of AIDS-related illness. The loss of her brother, whom she has described as one of her closest friends, affected her deeply, inspiring her second collection of poetry, *What the Living Do*. Her other published collections include *The Good Thief*, *The Kingdom of Ordinary Time* and, most recently, *Magdalene: Poems*. She also coedited *In the Company of My Solitude: American Writing from the AIDS Pandemic*. Marie Howe's poems have appeared in The New Yorker, The Atlantic, Poetry, Agni, Ploughshares, Harvard Review, and The Partisan Review. She was the Poet Laureate of New York State from 2012 to 2014.

Issa (Japan, 1763 – 1828)

Kobayashi Nobuyuki was a lay Buddhist priest and one of the great haiku masters. He adopted the pen name Issa, which means "a single cup of tea." Although Issa's life was filled with struggles—the death of his mother at an early age, conflicts with his stepmother, poverty, and the death of his own children—his haiku celebrate the serenity of pure moments in life.

Jacopone da Todi (Italy, 1230 – 1306)

Jacopone Benedetti was born to a family of means in the town of Todi, Italy. As a young man he began a career as a *notario*, combining the skills of an accountant and a lawyer. He also married young, but his life drastically changed when a balcony collapsed at a feast, mortally wounding his young wife. Devastated, he abandoned his career and gave away all of his possessions. For a while he became a wandering penitent and eventually joined the Franciscan order. Among the Franciscans, he discovered his gift for poetry. Brother Jacopone became a leader of the Spirituals faction of Franciscans who dedicated themselves to the ideal of radical poverty. Caught up in the ugly politics of papal succession of the time, he was imprisoned for five years for his opposition to the election of Pope Boniface VIII. Throughout this time, he continued to write his ecstatic poems on divine love. With his release on Pope Boniface's death, Jacopone retired to a hermitage near Orvieto. He died on Christmas Day in 1306.

John of the Cross (Spain, 1542 – 1591)
John of the Cross was raised in poverty by his widowed mother. In his early 20s, he entered the Carmelite Order and soon after met the woman who would become his mentor, Teresa of Avila. Teresa of Avila had begun a reform movement within their monastic order, advocating a return to simplicity and essential spirituality. John of the Cross joined her Discalced Carmelites and quickly became a leading figure within the movement. Other Carmelites felt threatened by the new movement, and they turned to force, capturing and imprisoning John of the Cross. It was in prison that John began to write poetry on smuggled scraps of paper. He escaped after nine months of imprisonment. John spent the rest of his life as a spiritual director among the Discalced Carmelites. His two best known works, the *Spiritual Canticle* and *Dark Night of the Soul*, are considered masterpieces of Spanish poetry and esoteric Christianity.

Jnaneshwar (India, 1275 – 1296)
The name Jnaneshwar (or Jnaneshvar) implies the realization of the Supreme Self, which is one with God (Ishwara) through gnosis (jnana). He is also known as Jnanadev, which suggests a similar meaning. When Jnaneshwar was a child, his father left the family to become a spiritual renunciate, but he later returned to care for his family at his guru's insistence. This family drama was shocking to orthodox authorities and the family was shunned. Soon after, when the children were still quite young, both parents died, and the children had to survive by begging. Yet from this impoverished family a spiritual vision of the greatest depth emerged: Not only did Jnaneshwar become a celebrated sage and poet while still a youth, his sister, Muktabai, also became a greatly revered poet-saint. Traditionally Jnaneshwar is said to have felt he had fulfilled his life purpose and left the body in *mahasamadhi* (supreme spiritual union at death), consciously exiting his body at the young age of 22. By then he had already been acknowledged as a great saint, philosopher, and poet.

Omar Khayyam (Persia/Iran, 1048 – 1131)
Omar Khayyam was a mathematician and astronomer. His quatrains (or *rubaiyat*) are commonly read in the West as a collection of sensual love poems. Although the question is still debated, Persian tradition asserts that Khayyam was a Sufi and his *Rubaiyat* can only be properly understood as spiritual metaphor.

Ko Un (Korea, 1933 –)
Ko Un was a witness to the devastation of the Korean War. He volunteered for the People's Army but was rejected because he was underweight. He became a Zen Buddhist monk in the 1950s and returned to secular life sometime in the 1960s. Ko Un became an activist opposing the harsh and arbitrary rule of the South Korean government of the time. His dissident activities led to several terms of imprisonment and torture. The democratization of South Korea in the late 1980s finally gave Ko Un the freedom to travel to other countries, allowing him to visit the United States and make a spiritual journey through India. He is married and has a daughter.

Lalla (Kashmir [India/Pakistan], 14th century)

Little is known for certain about the life of Lalla (also respectfully referred to as Lal Ded or Lalleshwari), other than hints that come to us through her poetry and songs. It is thought that she was born near Srinagar to an educated family. Tradition says she was a young bride forced into an unhappy marriage in which she was abused by her husband's family. While still a young woman, she left the marriage and took up the life of a wandering holy woman, singing songs of enlightenment to her beloved god Shiva. Her poems exhort us to seek the truth directly by looking within. Lalla's *vakhs* (versified sayings) have been cherished in Kashmir and passed down through oral tradition. They were only written down for the first time in the early 20th century.

Antonio Machado (Spain, 1763 – 1828)

Antonio Machado's poetry discovers revelation in the rural landscape and in the yearning of the human heart. Machado's wife died when she was very young. His lifelong anguish over this loss enters his poetry as a sort of private communion. His wife is ever with him, yet just out of reach, beckoning him to broader awareness.

Nirmala (US, contemporary)

Nirmala is a contemporary spiritual teacher in the nondualist Advaita tradition. He traces his spiritual lineage through Neelam and H.W.L. Poonja to Ramana Maharshi. Nirmala conducts regular satsangs in Arizona and teaches throughout the United States and other countries.

Ojibway (US)

The Ojibway (Chippewa) are one of the most numerous nations of Native Americans. Traditional Ojibway lands are centered in Michigan, Minnesota, Saskatchewan and surrounding regions.

Layman P'ang (China, 740? – 808)

P'ang Yun, popularly known as Layman P'ang, famously rejected the life of a monk even after attaining enlightenment, choosing instead to remain a common "layman." That act opened the way for subsequent generations of non-monastic seekers and householder sages. He did, however, reject wealth and worldly attachments as a snare. He was prosperous in his youth, but he worried too much about his wealth, so he decided to rid himself of it. Initially, he planned to give his wealth away, but then thought that whoever received his wealth would become as attached to it as he had. So, according to the stories, he piled all his worldly goods on a boat, floated it out to the middle of a lake, and sank it. After that, he and his family lived a modest life, supporting themselves by making bamboo utensils. *The Sayings of Layman P'ang* is an important Chinese Zen / Ch'an classic, a collection of short dialogues and poems.

Rabia al-Adawiyya (Persia/Iraq, 717 – 801)

Rabia al-Adawiyya, also referred to as Rabia of Basra or Rabia al-Basri, was born to a poor family in Basra in what is now Iraq. When she was young her parents died of famine and she was sold into slavery. The story is told that her master woke up one night and saw a light shining above her head while she was praying. Stunned, he freed her the next morning. Rabia chose a solitary life of prayer, living much of her life in desert seclusion. Her fame as a holy woman spread, and today she is greatly revered by devout Muslims and seekers of many religious traditions.

Ramprasad (India/Bengal, 1718? – 1775?)

Ramprasad Sen was born outside of Kolkata (Calcutta) in Bengal. Although a bright youth, he showed no interest in the family profession of Ayurveda. His focus on spiritual practices worried his parents, who were afraid he would renounce worldly life. To head off that possibility, his parents quickly married their otherworldly son to a young girl. Soon after the marriage, Ramprasad's father died, leaving the family in poverty. As the oldest son, the responsibility fell on Ramprasad to provide for the entire family. He found work as an accountant's clerk in Kolkata. But he couldn't prevent his devotional impulses from pouring out in the form of poetry. Lacking good paper, he wrote his poems in the margins of his account ledger. The office manager, upon reading Ramprasad's poems, was so moved that he told Ramprasad to go home and devote all his time to writing, reassuring him that he would still be paid his salary. Ramprasad regularly sang his songs to the Goddess Kali while immersed, neck-deep in the Ganges. A local prince overheard him one day and was so impressed that he appointed Ramprasad as his court poet, granting him land to support his family. Ramprasad's poetry to the Mother Goddess Kali is playful, petulant, blissful, sometimes even angry, expressing the tempestuous relationship between a child and his Mother, between the soul and the Eternal. By communicating everything to the Mother, he achieves a profound intimacy with the Divine.

Mevlana Jelaluddin Rumi (Persia/Afghanistan & Turkey, 1207 – 1273)

Rumi was born in the eastern end of the Persian Empire in what is today Afghanistan. While he was still a boy, his family fled the Mongol invasions and settled in Asia Minor (Turkey). Rumi was already a man with religious position when he encountered the wandering *dervish* Shams, who became his spiritual teacher. This meeting ignited a spiritual revolution within Rumi, his community, and his poetry, a revolution that reaches into the present day.

Santoka (Japan, 1882 – 1940)

Santoka Taneda is an intriguing figure who bridged ancient and modern Zen traditions in Japan at the beginning of the 20th century. He lived much of his life as a wandering hermit, taking to the road, visiting pilgrimage spots, begging, and composing haiku. He wrote, "Days I don't enjoy: Any day I don't walk, drink sake, and compose haiku." His haiku whittle down each moment to the observed bare essentials, witnessing the splendor in each mundane moment as it is.

Mahmud Shabistari (Persia/Iran, 1250? – 1340)

Mahmud Shabistari lived in Persia (Iran) during the time of the Mongol invasions. It was a terrible time of massacres, yet it is also during this time that the Golden Age of Persian Sufism emerged. Shabistari's *Secret Rose Garden* is considered to be one of the finest works of Persian Sufism. His poetry expresses a unified vision of reality using the elegant language of the Persian poetic tradition.

Shabkar (Tibet, 1781 – 1851)

Shabkar (or Shapkar) Tsogdruk Rangdrol was born in northeastern Tibet. As a youth, he resisted pressure from his family to marry and devoted himself to spiritual practice, taking monastic ordination at 21. He took up the life of a wandering hermit, traveling for the next thirty years to sacred sites and pilgrimage destinations. His life as an itinerant holy man and his songs of spiritual insight became widely known, earning him comparisons with the great Buddhist yogi-poet Milarepa. Shabkar was a nature mystic, conversing with sky and mountain and tree, seeing in them the embodiment of universal truths. Like St. Francis of Assisi, he is particularly famous for his love of animals.

Shankara (India, 788 – 820)

Shankara (referred to reverently as Adi Shankara or Shankaracharya) was an important philosopher, sage, holy man, religious reformer, and poet who unified nondualist philosophy, returning it to its central place within Hinduism. Shankara traveled extensively, engaging in philosophical debates and spreading essential truths on the nature of reality. He is also remembered for reorganizing monastic practice within Hinduism, and many monastic lineages trace their roots back to Adi Shankaracharya as their founder.

Symeon the New Theologian (Byzantine Empire/Turkey, 949 – 1032)

Symeon was born into an aristocratic family and, as a young man, he rose to the post of imperial senator. Yet his public life was in conflict with his inner life. Symeon left the senate and became a monk and a priest, eventually taking on the role of abbot. The mystical practices he advocated led to conflicts with church authorities, but eager students flocked to him. Today, he is one of the most important spiritual figures of the Eastern Orthodox Church.

Tulsi Sahib (India, 1763 – 1843)

Although Tulsi Sahib lived relatively recently, few details about his life can be stated with certainty. He may have been part of the royal family of Pune, India. One biographical account suggests he was engaged to be married against his will. On the day before the wedding, he ran away and took up the life of a spiritual mendicant who wandered through forests, going from town to town, engaged in meditation. In the early 1800s, he settled in Uttar Pradesh in northern India, where he spent the rest of his life. Tulsi Sahib practiced Surat Shabd Yoga, or the Yoga of Sound. He is particularly revered within the Sant Mat Sikh tradition.

Henry Vaughan (Wales, 1621 – 1695)

Amidst the English Civil War, Vaughan had a powerful mystical conversion, which he links to the inspired poetry of George Herbert. But, in contrast to Herbert's praises, Vaughan was more immediate and overtly mystical in his writing. His poetry describes ecstatic states of divine communion and a keen affinity for the natural world. Vaughan became a respected physician. He published his collected metaphysical poetry under the title *Silex Scintillans* (The Sparking Flint).

Dorothy Walters (United States, 1928 –)

Dorothy Walters, Ph.D., helped to set up one of the first women's studies programs in the country and was active in the early feminist and gay liberation movements. In 1981 she experienced a dramatic spiritual transformation through spontaneous *Kundalini* awakening. Since then, she has focused on writing about the spiritual journey, while helping to guide others who are undergoing similar experiences of transformation.

Walt Whitman (United States, 1819 – 1892)

Walt Whitman grew up in Brooklyn and Long Island. He trained as a printer from the age of twelve. He learned to love the written word and read all he could. In his late teens he became a teacher, then turned to journalism in his 20s, briefly moving to New Orleans as editor of a local newspaper. Having witnessed the cruelties of slavery in the South, he returned to Brooklyn as a confirmed abolitionist. Whitman self-published the first edition of what would come to be seen as his masterpiece, *Leaves of Grass*, in 1855, revising it several times in subsequent years. During the American Civil War, Whitman worked as a reporter and aided the wounded in local hospitals. Whitman struggled financially for many years, but with the successful publication of the 1882 edition of *Leaves of Grass* he finally began to earn enough money to purchase a house and live comfortably through his final years.

William Wordsworth (England, 1770 – 1850)

The Romantic poetry of William Wordsworth discovers meditative insights and transcendence amidst the natural world. Wordsworth was born to a prosperous family in the scenic Lake District of northwest England. His mother died while he was still a child. Prior to graduation from Cambridge, Wordsworth took a walking tour of Europe, reveling in the beauty of the Alps. Among his most loved poems are "Tintern Abbey," "Ode: Intimations of Immortality from Recollections of Early Childhood," and "The Prelude." In 1843 Wordsworth was named England's Poet Laureate.

Wu Men (China, 1183 – 1260)

Wu Men Huikai (known in Japanese as Mumon Ekai) was head monk of the Longxiang monastery in China and the author of one of the two most important collections of Zen koans, *The Gateless Gate* (Chinese: *Wu Men Kuan*; Japanese: *Mumonkan*). First published in 1228, *The Gateless Gate* consists of 48 koans compiled by Wu Men with his commentary and poetic verse.

Yoka Genkaku (China, 665 – 713)

Yongjia Xuanjue (best known in the West by his Japanese name, Yoka Genkaku) lived in south-eastern China. While still a youth, he left his home and began to practice meditation and study Buddhist texts. It is said that he received enlightenment upon reading the *Vimalakirti Nirdesha Sutra*. He is perhaps best known for composing *The Shodoka* (*Cheng Tao Ko*), a collection of Zen teaching poems, popularized in the West through the spread of Japanese Zen.

Acknowledgments

I wish to sincerely thank everyone who helped to bring this anthology to completion:

My wife, Michele Anderson, for her encouragement and vision.

My international band of keen-eyed proofreaders. Your diligence, patience, and willingness to mark up my manuscript helped immeasurably.

And, of course, the Poetry Chaikhana community. Your support and enthusiasm over the years helped bring this book into being. Thank you!

—⁓⁓—

Thanks also to the following poets, translators, and publishers for their generous permission to include their work in this collection.

Abu-Said Abil-Kheir, "The sum total of our life" and "The jewel of understanding" English versions by Vraje Abramian. Originally published in *Nobody, Son of Nobody: Poems of Shaikh Abu-Saeed Abil-Kheir* (Hohm Press). Used by permission of the publisher.

Ansari, "Give Me" English version by Andrew Harvey. Originally published in *Perfume of the Desert: Inspirations from Sufi Wisdom* (Quest Books). Used by permission.

"Arapaho Ghost Dance Songs" English version by James Mooney. Originally published in *Native American Songs and Poems: An Anthology*, edited by Brian Swann (Dover Thrift Editions). Used by permission.

Basho, "awakened" English version by Gabriel Rosenstock. Originally published in *Haiku Enlightenment* (Cambridge Scholars Publishing). Used by permission.

Constantine P. Cavafy, "Ithaca" English version by Ivan M. Granger.

Chiyo-ni, "whatever I pick up" English version by Gabriel Rosenstock. Originally published in *Haiku Enlightenment* (Cambridge Scholars Publishing). Used by permission.

Andrew Colliver, "Come" Used by permission of the author.

Dionysius the Areopagite, "Lead us up beyond light" English version by Ivan M. Granger.

Dogen, "Worship" English version by Ivan M. Granger.

Johann Wolfgang von Goethe, "What is this dance of bliss?" and "Green is the tree of life" English versions by Ivan M. Granger.

Zeynep Hatun, "I am a fountain, You are my water" English version by Murat Yagan. Originally published in *Women of Sufism: A Hidden Treasure, Writings and Stories of Mystic Poets, Scholars & Saints*, edited by Camille Adams Helminski (Shambhala). Used by the kind permission of the translator and Kebzeh Publications.

Hildegard von Bingen, "Laus Trinitati" English version by Ivan M. Granger.

Friedrich Holderlin, "The fruits are ripened" English version by Ivan M. Granger

Marie Howe, "Annunciation" selection from "Poems from the Life of Mary" originally published in *The Kingdom of Ordinary Time* (W. W. Norton and Company). Used by permission of the author.

Issa, "stillness" English version by David G. Lanoue. Originally published on The Haiku of Kobayashi Issa website *www.haikuguy.com/issa/*. Used by permission of the translator. "In my hut" English version by Gabriel Rosenstock. Originally published in *Haiku Enlightenment* (Cambridge Scholars Publishing).

Jacopone da Todi, "As air carries light" English version by Ivan M. Granger.

Jnaneshwar, "The Union of Shiva and Shakti" English version by Swami Abhayananda. Originally published in *Jnaneshvar: The Life and Works of the Celebrated Thirteenth Century Indian Mystic-Poet* (Atma Books). Used by permission.

John of the Cross, "I Entered the Unknown" English version by Ivan M. Granger.

Ko Un, "Two beggars" English version by Brother Anthony of Taize. Used by permission.

Lalla, "Held fast in winter's fist" English version by Ivan M. Granger.

Antonio Machado, "Hope says" English version by Ivan M. Granger.

Nirmala, "words do not come" Originally published in *Gifts with No Giver: A Love Affair with Truth* (CreateSpace). Used by permission of the author.

"Ojibway Song" English version by Ivan M. Granger.

Layman P'ang, "The mind is a reflection in the mirror" English version by Ivan M. Granger.

Rabia al-Adawiyya, "Through and Through" English version by Ivan M. Granger. Originally published in *Diamond Cutters: Visionary Poets in America, Britain & Oceania*, edited by Andrew Harvey and Jay Ramsay (Tayen Lane Publishing).

Ramprasad, "Mind, don't you sleep" Translated by Leonard Nathan and Clinton Seely. Originally published in *Grace and Mercy in Her Wild Hair: Selected Poems to the Mother Goddess* (Hohm Press). Used by permission of the publisher.

Mevlana Jelaluddin Rumi, "Fasting" and "Whoever finds love" (excerpted and versified from "Dying, Laughing") English versions © Coleman Barks. Originally published in *The Essential Rumi* (HarperOne). Reprinted by permission of Coleman Barks. "look at love" English version by Nader Khalili. Originally published in *Rumi: Fountain of Fire* (Cal-Earth Press). Reprinted by permission of the publisher. "The Lion, the Wolf, and the Fox" English version by Ivan M. Granger.

Santoka, "Hailstones, too" English version by John Stevens. Originally published in *Mountain Tasting: The Haiku and Journals of Santoka Taneda* (White Pine Press). Used by permission of the publisher.

Shabkar, "The mind has neither color nor form" English version by Matthieu Ricard. Originally published in *Rainbows Appear: Tibetan Poems of Shabkar* (Shambhala). Used by permission. "Among mountain caves" English version by Ivan M. Granger.

Shankara, "You are my true self, O Lord" English version by Ivan M. Granger.

Symeon the New Theologian, "The fire rises in me" English version by Ivan M. Granger. Originally published in *Real Thirst: Poetry of the Spiritual Journey* (Poetry Chaikhana).

Tulsi Sahib, "Within this body" English version by Ivan M. Granger. Originally published in *Real Thirst: Poetry of the Spiritual Journey* (Poetry Chaikhana).

Dorothy Walters, "Preparing to Greet the Goddess" Originally published in *Unmasking the Rose: A Record of a Kundalini Initiation* (Hampton Roads). Used by permission of the author.

Wu Men, "A hundred flowers in spring" and "Tipping Over a Vase" English versions by Ivan M. Granger.

Yoka Genkaku (Yongjia Xuanjue), "Right here it is eternally full and serene" excerpt from *The Shodoka (Cheng Tao Ko)*. Translated by Robert Aitken, Roshi © 2016 The Honolulu Diamond Sangha. Thanks to the Honolulu Diamond Sangha for permission to reprint. "When all is finally seen as it is" English version by Ivan M. Granger.

Made in the USA
Columbia, SC
16 February 2021

33011866R00107